COMPUTER SCIENCE, TECHNOLOGY AND APPLICATIONS

GESTURE RECOGNITION

PERFORMANCE, APPLICATIONS AND FEATURES

Computer Science, Technology and Applications

Additional books in this series can be found on Nova's website under the Series tab.

Additional e-books in this series can be found on Nova's website under the e-book tab.

COMPUTER SCIENCE, TECHNOLOGY AND APPLICATIONS

GESTURE RECOGNITION

PERFORMANCE, APPLICATIONS AND FEATURES

GILBERTO COLEMAN
AND
ROOSEVELT WARD
EDITORS

nova
science publishers
New York

NOTICE TO THE READER

Library of Congress Cataloging-in-Publication Data

Names: Coleman, Gilberto, editor. | Ward, Roosevelt, editor.
Title: Gesture recognition : performance, applications and features / Gilberto Coleman and Roosevelt Ward, editors.
Description: Hauppauge, New York : Nova Science Publishers, Inc., [2018] | Series: Computer science, technology and applications | Includes bibliographical references and index.
Identifiers: LCCN 2018017588 (print) | LCCN 2018019848 (ebook) | ISBN 9781536134926 (ebook) | ISBN 9781536134919 (softcover) | ISBN 9781536134926 (ebook)
Subjects: LCSH: Human face recognition (Computer science) | Gesture. | Human-computer interaction.
Classification: LCC TA1653 (ebook) | LCC TA1653 .G47 2018 (print) | DDC 006.4--dc23
LC record available at https://lccn.loc.gov/2018017588

Published by Nova Science Publishers, Inc. † New York

CONTENTS

PREFACE

In the opening chapter of *Gesture Recognition: Performance, Applications and Features*, the authors discuss gesture recognition and its role in the developing world of technology. The possibility of implementing a gesture detection application that works with people with special needs is examined, such as recognition of sign language for the hearing-impaired. Following this, the authors present their approach for face detection and tracking, user identification, facial feature extraction and head pose estimation as the low-level representation of facial gesture atomics. Additionally, an approach for a movement-based facial gestures recognition is presented, with results demonstrated through practical approaches. A later work explores spectral features from algebraic graph theory in static hand gesture recognition. Specifically, the authors apply a technique that uses the elements of the spectral matrix of the Laplacian to construct symmetric polynomials that are permutation invariants. The values of these polynomials can be used as graph features in a statistical learning pipeline that has the ability of distinguishing between distinct graphs and can reveal graph clusters. In the closing study, the authors developed two algorithms for the detection of pointing gestures and one approach for waving on this technological base and studied their functionality. The goal was to determine whether a combination of both strategies improves and stabilizes detection rates.

Chapter 1 - With the advancement and development of technology in recent years, multimedia devices have become even smarter. The devices are now equipped with multiple camera sensors and depth sensors. All these devices require a real-time computer user interface. In recent years, other devices such as mechanical gloves and systems have been introduced to monitor the user's movements.

One of the most interesting areas is the use of gestures to interact with the computer or device. However, the hand model provides information about the location and other hand features when detecting the gesture. This makes the programming complex and creates several difficulties in monitoring.

To develop an application is essential to study gestures. There are many gestures that are used to interact with a physical interface. Some of these are the movements of the fingers of the hands and the body in general. Also, the direction of the glances can be seen as a gesture as well as the expressions of the person. Gestures are graded based on the importance of the gesture, the gesture function, and the description of the operation.

To monitor tracking or to implement a program, one of the key goals is to use new technologies that make the system easy to use and at low cost. Some of the commercially available technologies that also provide us with the ability to recognize gestures are Kinect and Leap Motion. Basic differences in technology are distinguished by the distance between user and computer. Much of the available software is being studied and can be used to detect a gesture. When a company develops and creates a new proprietary technology, it initially tries to secure control and rights. However, many companies have a different policy and there are many business platforms that remain available to the general public. In order to help the use of technology for innovation and growth in other industries, companies have left free software. For example, in Leap Motion there is an SDK library that provides the user with easy programming. In addition, many ready-to-use applications are provided. Some industries that use motion detection technology are medical, robotics, intelligent agent and environmental industries.

The choice of technology and applications is rapid. The technology offers many possibilities and many aspirations and expectations for the near future. The authors must be able to follow it and discover it. In the next pages, the authors will go into the world of technology and they will discover how they can implement their own gesture detection application that also serves people with special needs, such as the recognition of sign language.

Chapter 2 - Computer based facial gesture recognition became a field of intense interest in human-computer interactions recently. The aim of this field of science is to translate several facial information into a human-like and human-interpretable description in order to communicate with computers in a more natural way. The domain of facial gesture recognition problems can be defined easily, however the algorithms should work beside various facial positions, orientations and appearances that can result a considerable obstacle in the implementation. The first step of facial gesture recognition is the determination of those atomics that are relevant in production of the facial gestures themselves. Such atomics are the location of the face; the position of several facial feature points; the spatial position and orientation of the face or head; the changes in location or appearance taking place in time. This chapter presents the authors' approach for face detection and tracking, user identification, facial feature extraction and head pose estimation as the low-level representation of facial gesture atomics. At a higher level, the authors give an approach for a movement based facial gestures recognition and they demonstrate their results through practical approaches as some applications of facial gesture recognition.

Chapter 3 - In this work, the main goal is to explore spectral features from algebraic graph theory in static hand gesture recognition. Specifically, the authors apply a technique that uses the elements of the spectral matrix of the Laplacian to construct symmetric polynomials that are permutation invariants. The values of these polynomials can be used as graph features in a statistical learning pipeline that has the ability of distinguishing between distinct graphs and can reveal graph clusters. This technique avoids the correspondences between the nodes of graphs. So, the authors take a set of hand gestures RGB images and perform their segmentation through a graph-cuts algorithm. The obtained regions are processed for key points extraction. Next, the authors represent each hand region with a graph in order to compute the spectral features. In this case, the authors can compare the feature vectors, computed for different hand poses, using the Euclidean metric. The sensitivity of spectral features against graph changes will be considered in the corresponding experiments. Next, the authors evaluate the spectral features ability to group different gestures as different graph clusters. The results point toward the necessity of embedding the graph feature vectors in a compact space, computed by principal components analysis (PCA), followed by the linear discriminant analysis (LDA) technique to calculate the more important directions for classification. Using this approach the authors get suitable recognition rates for two class separating problems using K-nearest-neighbor (KNN) classifier. However, the authors notice a decreasing in the accuracy for multi-class problems indicating the necessity of improvements in the recognition methodology.

Chapter 4 - To make use of gesture detection in HMI, algorithms for their occurrence in working processes should be defined. Since affordable motion capturing devices like Microsoft® Kinect® in science and industry were proved to be simply applicable in working environments, the authors developed and studied the functionality of two algorithms for the detection of pointing gestures, and one approach for waving on this technological base.

The "phase model" of speech supporting gestures by McNeill (1992) proposes to structure a gesture into three (optional five) phases. This phase model is the base of a technical description, which can be shown to be able to automatically detect "pointing" and "waving."

Differing static and dynamic gestures, detection rates are up to 85%, if the interacting human turns less than 30° in relation to the frontal aspect of the MS® Kinect® sensor. In pointing gestures "static" was identified to mean that the body posture should be kept for about 0.5 seconds. If the pointing algorithm rejects a gesture as "not pointing," the motion is checked for resembling "waving." "Waving" is characterized by a dynamic (periodic) stroke phase which may be detected by a frequency analysis (FFT), without any necessity of keeping positions.

At the present state, having analyzed 1073 recorded gesture sequences, the "static pointing algorithm" provides a detection rate of about 53%, the "phase-based approach for pointing" a detection rate of about 86%, and the "waving algorithm" a detection rate of about 82%. In a parallel project, in structured environment algorithms for pointing reached 92% detection rate using stochastic approaches. But this strategy turned out to be very sensitive to changes of the environment, while the above described deterministic approaches proved to be rather robust. Whether a combination of both strategies improves and stabilizes detection rates, is under study.

In: Gesture Recognition
Editors: G. Coleman and R. Ward
ISBN: 978-1-53613-491-9

Chapter 1

GESTURE RECOGNITION

Despoina Kotsidou
Software Engineer,
Technological Educational Institute, Vienna, Austria

ABSTRACT

With the advancement and development of technology in recent years, multimedia devices have become even smarter. The devices are now equipped with multiple camera sensors and depth sensors. All these devices require a real-time computer user interface. In recent years, other devices such as mechanical gloves and systems have been introduced to monitor the user's movements.

One of the most interesting areas is the use of gestures to interact with the computer or device. However, the hand model provides information about the location and other hand features when detecting the gesture. This makes the programming complex and creates several difficulties in monitoring.

To develop an application is essential to study gestures. There are many gestures that are used to interact with a physical interface. Some of these are the movements of the fingers of the hands and the body in general. Also, the direction of the glances can be seen as a gesture as well as the expressions of the person. Gestures are graded based on the importance of the gesture, the gesture function, and the description of the operation.

To monitor tracking or to implement a program, one of the key goals is to use new technologies that make the system easy to use and at low cost. Some of the commercially available technologies that also provide us with the ability to recognize gestures are Kinect and Leap Motion. Basic differences in technology are distinguished by the distance between user and computer. Much of the available software is being studied and can be used to detect a gesture. When a company develops and creates a new proprietary technology, it initially tries to secure control and rights. However, many companies have a different policy and there are many business platforms that remain available to the general public. In order to help the use of technology for innovation and growth in other industries, companies have left free software. For example, in Leap Motion there is an SDK library that provides the user with easy programming. In addition, many ready-to-use applications are provided. Some industries that use motion detection technology are medical, robotics, intelligent agent and environmental industries.

The choice of technology and applications is rapid. The technology offers many possibilities and many aspirations and expectations for the near future. We must be able to follow it and discover it. In the next pages, we will go into the world of technology and we will discover how we can implement our own gesture detection application that also serves people with special needs, such as the recognition of sign language.

Keywords: kinect, leap motion, assisted living technology, hand gesture recognition, application based systems

Introduction

Communication between people requires the use of various means of expression. People use different expressions such as speech, gestures, look, facial expression, and body posture. In this way, communication between people is achieved either by combining these expressions or individually. By enabling the user to use everyday communications to interact with the computer, we achieve a more anthropocentric design. The human-to-computer interface can make communication even easier. To do this, however, we need the right technology that should be accessible to the average user, such as the microphone and camera that act as input devices;

with the proper processing, they satisfy some of the abovementioned modes of expression, such as speech or facial expression. But to identify the movement of the human body, we need different and more specialized equipment.

Motion detection is a process that confirms the change in the position of an object relative to its environment or the change in the surrounding area relative to an object. This detection can be achieved by mechanical (keyboard keys) as well as electronic (camera, microphone, infrared, laser) methods. Motion detection can either be discrete or obvious, i.e., if there was movement or not (1 or 0). Motion can be detected by: sound (acoustic sensors), opacity (optical and infrared sensors, and video processors), reflection of the transferred energy (infrared laser radars, ultrasonic sensors and microwave radar sensors), electromagnetic induction (inductive loop detectors), and vibration (triboelectric, seismic, etc.).

Movement is defined in physics as the change in the position or orientation of a body relative to a given reference system. The reference system is considered to be attached to a body (or body system) which we consider as contractually immobile. Therefore, we can abusively talk about the movement of one body in relation to another body.

If the body changes position, we say it moves. But it moves in relation to a reference point. The move is therefore relative, that is, it refers to a point or body that is considered stationary.

In the next section, we will deal with locating the traffic. To do this, we will study and analyze available equipment. There are two available types of software that we can use. The first is Microsoft Kinect and the second is Leap Motion.

The goal is to get to know Microsoft Kinect and Leap Motion and compare these two technologies. We will present an architecture that uses natural (human) expression methods to interact with the computer, making the interface more natural. In this way, the degree of difficulty in adapting the user to the system will be greatly reduced, while the system will be quite flexible for users with weaknesses in some of the natural expression methods.

We will look at the Microsoft Kinect and Leap Motion input devices. We will then study and compare the API libraries of both technologies, capabilities and programming languages that enable us to program, according to the application we are interested in. In addition, we will analyze the applications that use Microsoft Kinect and Leap Motion, such as virtual reality, robotics, medicine and disabilities (such as deafness) as well as motion recognition.

1. Study of Gestures and Detection of Hand Movement Patterns

Gestures are the product of the interaction between humans and consist of movements of the body and the person, which replace the oral communication. Gestures are essential for natural and authentic human communication. Naturally some interfaces can use strong gestures. The design of gesture-based interfaces is quite difficult since the creation of gesture patterns stems from the natural movements of man, which are quite complex in several cases.

There are many gestures that are used to interact with a physical interface. Some of these are the movements of the fingers of the hands and the body in general.

Also, the direction of the look can be considered as a gesture as well as facial expressions.

The classification of gestures is based on:

- The importance of the gesture where you relate to the communication and purpose of that movement. These gestures are divided into:
    - Conscious, meaningful even if not followed by speech. Conscious gestures are the ones that play the key role in the physical user interface.

- Spontaneous, which must be accompanied by speech to make sense. These gestures need multimodal interfaces that can support their entry in addition to movement and speech.
- The operation of the gesture describing its effect on an interface. The gestures based on their function are divided into:
    - Command orders, which give access to system operations.
    - Direct gestures, where they are used to select objects on an interface.
    - Manual manipulations necessary to manage and process two-dimensional or 3D objects, such as rotating a 3D image.
    - Control chronologies that are related to the control of an object, such as a camera.
- The description of the gesture that has to do with how it is performed and what are the necessary moves. These gestures are used in:
    - Static, which require a specific position of the hands and fingers without taking into account any movement.
    - Dynamic, which is based on motion without time being the role.
    - Space-time, which is essentially a sub-category of dynamics and associated with continuous movement within a certain time.

1.1. Natural User Interface

In the 1990s Steve Mann (1962)[1] was recognized as “the father of wearable computing” and “her father’s University of Toronto and President of IEEE Technology and Society”, developed a series of user interface strategies using physical interaction with the real world as an alternative to a CLI and graphical interface (GUI). Steve Mann referred to this project as natural user interfaces (Interfaces).

[1] Steve Mann (1962) has been recognized as “the father of wearable computing” and “her father University of Toronto and President of the IEEE Technology and Society”.

In 2006, an open research community, Christian Moore, was set up to explore NUI-related development. At the 2008 "Predicting the Past" conference, Microsoft described NUI technology as the next evolutionary stage after switching from CLI to GUI

In 2010 Bill Buxton, one of the pioneers in multipath technology and more generally in the field of physical interfaces, gave the following theoretical physics interface:

> *"An interface is considered natural when it exploits the skills it has acquired from the experience of its life in the natural world"*

1.1.1. The Term User Interface

The term user interface is the set of widgets of a system that appear on the screen of a digital device and allow two-way communication between that system and the user.

In computer science, a physical user interface, or NUI is the term used by designers and developers of human machine interfaces to refer to a user interface that is basically essentially invisible and secondly based on physical data. The word natural is used because most computer interfaces use artificial control devices whose functions should be trained. Interface requires learning, and this learning is facilitated by design that gives the user the feeling that communication is immediate and continually successful.

Components of the system hardware included in the user interface can be a contact screen, or a mouse. Parts of the user interface software are, for example, error messages, audio messages, navigation tools, symbol icons, and objects on the screen, everything the software has as a component of the system's interaction with the user. The term in terms of software of substance means a set of visual and acoustic parameters that the computer provides to the user, through the running of the program, for better communication and cooperation between man and machine.

"A physical user interface is an interface that is designed to reuse existing user skills and is designed to properly interact with the content."
Joshua Blake[2]

The term 'communication with the user' includes the concept of its interaction with the object. What the user can do with the object, and what the subject can do for the user, are parts of that communication. The usefulness of an object depends on the ability of the consumer to handle it successfully. If a user can not verify how an object works, then its communication with it is incomplete and the usability of the object is automatically considered to be unsuccessful.

For many years human-computer interaction has been done through tools such as mouse, keyboard or stylus. The physical user interface (NUI) in recent years has come to remove these devices as intermediaries and puts the physical functions of man, such as speech, motion and even thought, into the foreground as a direct way of interacting the user with the computer.

Most modern computer programs and operating systems offer their users GUI technology because this way of interacting with the computer fits well into human experience and nature. It has well designed graphics that offer a beautiful, easy-to-use and working interface.

However, the physical user interface will replace the graphical interface. As we have seen above, the graphical interfaces have largely replaced command line interfaces, however, there has not been a complete replacement of these interfaces since they are still used in management systems and programming tasks.

1.2. Multimodal Interfaces

Multimodal interfaces combine various ways of introducing the user, such as voice, stylus, touch, gestures, look, and head and body movement.

[2] Joshua Blake, Technical Director of InfoStrat Advanced Technology Group. Leader of the Natural User Interface, specializing in Kinect Interaction Design and Development. Trying to change how they interact with computers through innovative user interfaces.

They represent a new direction, deviating from standard graphical interfaces because they include recognition technologies designed to handle both contiguous and simultaneous inputs from parallel incoming channels, and to process input ambiguities by probabilistic methods, distributed processing and time-based architectures. These new kind of interfaces aims at recognizing human communication so that interaction with the computer is more natural to the user.

1.2.1. Benefits of User Interfaces

Robustness: Redundancy in multi-tropic input increases the quality of communication between the user and the system by assigning similar or associated information using different inputs, increasing the likelihood of recognition. Strategies of mutual clarification and integration of input data, in which integrated multi-tropic inputs are processed together, can help increase system performance.

Naturalness: Multi-tropical communication can lead to a great degree of naturalness, utilizing the established practices of human communication. Complex processes can be facilitated by multi-tropical interaction because the example effectively increases the bandwidth of communication between the user and the system by increasing the level of input expressivity.

Flexibility: A big advantage of multimodal interfaces is that they allows users to perceive and structure communication in a variety of ways depending on the environment. Users choose what modalities they will use and how they will be structured on the basis of semantic, time and drafting rules. Users have also shown a preference, in multi-tropical inputs, for orientated applications, however, they tend to alternate a self-tropical and multi-tropic interaction where they find it convenient.

Minimizing Errors: It has been shown that multi-tropical interfaces increase system performance by reducing the number of errors (through error avoidance) and the problems caused by spontaneous non-fluency speech compared to the interfaces that use voice recognition only for interactive applications that have space.

Multimodal user interfaces can also be better accessed. A well-designed, multimodal application can be used by people with various disabilities. Visually impaired users can use voice modality in combination with a keyboard. Users with hearing problems can use optical modality and voice input.

Users who have problems due to their situation (for example, those who use gloves in a noisy environment, drive or have to give their credit card code while in public) can also use the appropriate tropism.

1.2.2. Multimodal Entrance

Multimodal input systems to date are capable of processing two to three input channels, are specialized for some applications and have limited interaction vocabularies and grammar. The two most common types of multi-tropic input systems are the mouse and the keyboard that have been replaced by speech and the stylus.

Multimodal systems that include 3D gestures have made their appearance, however they are not as mature as compared to the technologies used to enter the stylus. The introduction of other input modes based on image capture devices such as look, facial expressions, head movements and body movements are of great interest in new types of interaction, which are still low.

Some of the input devices that are based on the physical user interface are:

1. Depth camera
2. Touch sensors
3. Depth sensors
4. Prime Sense Multi Sensor
5. Kinect Multi Sensor

1.2.3. Multimodal Exit

The second type of multimodal systems gives the user multimedia stimuli and multimodal output, mainly in the form of image or sound. It has begun to make use of other modes in designing interfaces such as touch and smell. Multimodal output systems have the following advantages: synergy and redundancy. The information presented in different ways operates in a single way and concerns different aspects of the same work. Using different modulations to process the same information results in a higher information transfer bandwidth.

Multimodal output is primarily used to improve matching between the media and content, and to manage attention in environments with a large volume of data where users need to have their attention focused.

An important step in the design of multimodal interfaces is the creation of physical mapping between modalities and information or tasks. Hearing differs from vision. It is not directional, it is transient and always works. Specifically, speech output, which is a form of audio information, is the subject of study and various techniques for the use of speech have been developed. Michaelis and Wiggins (1982) argued that speech output should be used for simple and short messages that will not be needed in the future. They also felt that it would be better for speech to be produced as soon as possible and to be answered by the user.

2. Kinect Technology

Kinect's history began before the Kinect mechanism was designed. Kinect has been rooted for decades where the user interface was based on gestures and voice. Based on this 2005 conference at the Tokyo Game Show, Nintendo made the unveiling of the Wii console. The console was accompanied by a new game from a new Wii Remote device. Like magnetic cubes, Wii Remote can detect 3D motion. In addition, the console contains an optical sensor where it detects movement. This software makes the vision a reality. It's not just a device with which you can play tennis with your friends, it's a 3-D video, it's part of the room.

Until recently, technologies such as depth and motion recording only existed in the workshops and in animated film studios where they used expensive and specialized equipment. With the emergence of low-cost deep sensor from PrimeSense, the hardware problem was solved and these capabilities came to the hands of everyday users as well as researchers from different fields.

On June 1, 2009, Microsoft announced a project called Project Natal that will allow the player to recognize the player's traffic on the Xbox 360. The name, like all Microsoft code names was given by a city. Brazil's Natal city was selected in honor of Brazilian director Alex Kipman, who was responsible for the project, and was originally from there. The second reason for this name was that the word natal means "birth", which they wanted to symbolize the birth of the new generation of entertainment at home. The name of the final product was Kinect from kinetic and connect. Kinect made its appearance in the market in November 2010. Two months after its release, Microsoft sold 8 million units, giving it the title of the fastest selling electronic device in the Guinness Book. 18 million Kinect had been sold by January 2012.

2.1. Skeleton Tracking

Skeleton Tracking is one of Kinect's most important functions. It allows Kinect to recognize human bodies and follow their movement. Using the infrared (IR) camera, Kinect can recognize up to two users, who are in front of Kinect, with detailed positioning and orientation information. In this way, it can locate the looks of localized users in the space and monitor their movements over time.

The data is provided in the application as a set of skeleton positions, which constitute a frame. This skeleton represents the position and posture of the body.

Skeleton detection is gradually being optimized to identify users in both upright and seated positions. In a standing position, the device recognizes twenty joints, and while sitting only ten, since many of these joints are under the Shoulder Center and are not visible in this posture.

In default range mode, Kinect can recognize people standing between 0.8 meters and 4.0 meters away from the sensor. Of course the practical distance for the smooth operation of the tracking is from 1.2 to 3.5 meters.

In near range mode, which is supported by SDK version 1.5, user skeletons can be identified from a closer distance of between 0.4 and 3 meters. Here it has to be said that Kinect for Xbox does not support Kinect for Xbox, but only Kinect for PC, which is estimated at about twice the price.

In combination with Skeleton Tracking and the joints resulting from this function, gestures can be used as a basic tool for determining physical type commands from users.

In conclusion, since a user's wrist may be monitored over a period of time, a command can be specified to move the user's hand from right to left within a certain amount of time. In addition, using this feature offered by Kinect, we can define with a code the location and movement of the user's fingers.

2.2. Kinect and APIs

On November 4, an electronics tool maker, Adafruit, announced that it would pay $1,000 to the first developer or the first programming team to develop a programming code for Kinect on Windows or another operating system, and to use Kinect in education or in robotics.

A few hours after this announcement of Adafruit's fee, Microsoft announced that it does not tolerate the modification of its products. Microsoft provides numerous hardware and software warranties designed to reduce the likelihood of tampering with and spoiling the product. Microsoft also said it would work closely with the principles of the law to keep Kinect inviolable.

That same afternoon Adafruit, the electronics tool maker, had doubled its pay to $2,000.

On Nov. 7, Microsoft Kinect was hacked by the hacker nicknamed AlexP who had managed to control Kinect's motorized base.

Image 1. Kinect for Windows.

Microsoft, to deny this event, announced that Kinect had not been hacked. Adafruit, after Microsoft's denial, wrote that it was raising the fee to $ 3,000.

Two days later AlexP published a video that showed he had control of the Kinect depth sensor and camera. The prize was his if he published the code. But publication of the code required $10,000.

On Wednesday, November 10, Héctor Martín, a hacker and computer science student, bought Kinect. Shortly after 11:00 am he communicated with Kinect, and had an image from the depth map and camera of the device on his screen. Héctor Martín published the source code for the use of Kinect on the Linux computer and Adafruit recognized him as the winner, giving him the $3,000 prize.

Then, other versions of his data decoded Kinect, resulting in the creation of several APIs with different capabilities.

2.2.1. Application Programming Interface (API)

The term API refers to the set of functions provided by a programming library to provide communication with the operating system or control program or device but without allowing access to the code.

2.2.2. Open Kinect

Héctor Martín, a computer hacker and student of science, published on November 10 the first library created to decode Kinect data. This library is Open Kinect or Libfreenect. Developed in C and Python, Libfreenect provides a large number of wrappers, in various languages, and the appropriate bibliography for their use. The library provides access to the camera, depth sensor, LED and motorized base of the device. A low-level API is characterized because beyond communication with the device, it does not provide methods such as Skeleton Tracking. But there are a large number of developers who use it, and it is commercially free to run on Windows, Mac OSX, and Linux.

2.2.3. CL NUI

The first version of the CL NUI platform was released on December 8, 2010 and is widely known in the robotics industry because it is the only library that gives access to the Kinect accelerometer. The CL NUI platform is based on the deinterlacing of Kinect's data by Alex P, but he did not immediately publish his code.

2.2.4. Open NI

It was created by a non-profit organization made up of several companies, including PrimeSence Ltd, who wanted to set up an industry standard for physical user interface devices (Natural User Interaction Devices) and released them in December 2010. OpenNI was developed in C/C ++ so it can be used by various operating systems such as Mac OSX, Ubuntu and Windows. It is the official X-ray device software of Asus, but it can also work with Kinect. It provides communication with the depth sensor, color camera, microphones, and power base. OpenNI, however, is also accompanied by an intermediate library called NITE and equipped with Voice Recognition, Hand Gesture Recognition, and Skeleton Detection.

Image 2. Skeleton Tracking with Open NI.

2.2.5. Microsoft Kinect for Windows SDK

The Windows Software Development Kit (SDK) is a set of libraries that allows program applications to deploy platforms using Kinect sensors as inputs. With the sensors, we can program WPF, Win Forms, and XNA applications. We can also program any Windows application. Kinect for (SDK) allows developers to create applications that support gesture and voice recognition by using Kinect sensor technology on Windows 7 and Windows 8 computers. Kinect for Windows SDK allows us to use C + +, C #, or Visual Basic to create applications and experiences that support gesture and voice recognition.

2.2.6. Evoluce SDK

The Evoluce SDK for Kinect allows developers to create applications even without experience. The SDK uses Speed Recognition, Finger Gesture Recognition as well as Surface support. Applications can also be used in areas such as events, exhibitions, education as well as health care.

The Evoluce SDK includes high quality technical support, such as the "Motor Sport" demo application. Users can navigate through a menu and have video and video control with simple hand movements. Users can take control by shaking hands while in the sensor area allowing interaction without a controller up to 4.5 m apart.

2.3. Compare APIs

Depending on the application we want to implement, we must also use the corresponding library to meet the requirements of the application with a view to its better and faster implementation. Above we have seen in detail the capabilities of the APIs, the functional ones from which they are supported, and the programming languages that we can use for each library.

In the table below we will look at API libraries and programming languages in which they are written and can be programmed.

2.4. Applications Using Kinect

When a company develops and creates a new proprietary technology, it initially tries to secure control and rights. This was Microsoft's initial move after Kinect's release. But soon it changed its policies. Microsoft created a business platform called "Kinect Accelerator" to help Kinect use innovation for other industries as well. As of July 2013, Kinect's technology has remained at the disposal of the general public. Some industries that use Kinect's technology and applications are Robotics, Virtual Reality, Intelligent Agent and Environment, and Medical and Disabilities.

Table 1. Compare APIs

	C/C++	C#	JAVA	PYTHON	VB. NET	JANASCRIPT
Open NI	√	√				
Libfreenect	√			√		
CL NUI	√	√				
MS Kinect SDK	√	√			√	
Evoluce SDK	√	√				

2.4.1. Robotics

Robotics is a branch of science that studies machines that can replace humans in performing a job. Robotics is a modern automation industry. The goal of automation is increased productivity, improved quality of life, and increased business profitability.

According to the definition of the US Robot Institute, "Robot is a reprogrammable multifunctional manipulator designed to move materials, parts, tools and specialized devices through variable, programmed movements to perform a series of tasks."

As mentioned above, they are the ones who use Kinect technology in various industries. One of them is the branch of robotics. Many companies have used Kinect's applications in conjunction with robotics to bring together interesting projects designed to facilitate everyday life.

Example 1

One of the most interesting projects is the combination of an iRobot Create (iRobot is known for Roomba robotic brooms and iRobot Create is a special edition made for robotics) and Kinect. This project is able to create a three-dimensional model of the space it is located in and sends it to a nearby computer, also trying to locate people in the area and understanding commands that are given through meanings. The project uses code from OpenSLAM for mapping and mapping placement in the space.

2.4.2. Virtual Reality

In 1989, the first definition of virtual reality was given by Jaron Lanier, the father of the term, who discusses virtual reality as "An interactive, three-dimensional, computer-based environment in which one can immerse."

The last conditions for virtual reality were given in 2003 and are as follows:

"The simulation of a real or imaginary environment that the user can experience visually in the three dimensions of width, height and depth and which can additionally provide an interactive real-time visual experience with sound and possibly tactile or other forms of feedback."

"A medium consisting of interactive computer simulations that" sense "the position and actions of the user, and replace or augment feedback in one or more senses, giving the feeling of spiritual immersion or presence in simulation (a virtual world)." Sherman, W.R., Craig, A., B.

The latter, in the scientific community, avoids the use of the term Virtual Reality because of its contradiction and uses the term Virtual Environment.

Example 1

IllumiRoom technology is the creation of the Microsoft Research Group, which creates accompanying visual "frames" within the player's site, based on the video game being played. In essence, a Kinect peripheral and an external projector are combined: Kinect "reads" the configuration of the room and then the system delivers the image to the projector. This image has real-time interactive features: e.g., in a big explosion that happens in the video game, the surrounding picture is disturbed.

2.4.3. Medical and Disabilities

Medicine is the science that deals with the research and implementation of methods on health issues. The aim is the prevention, diagnosis and treatment of human diseases.

The rapid development of Biomedical Imaging, Medical Informatics and Bioinformatics and the rapid expansion of their use in Health Sciences (Medicine, Biology, Biotechnology) aims to ensure a better quality of life for people with various problems (vision, hearing, disabilities). Another goal of medical technology is to provide the patient with less pain, minimize the likelihood of complications, reduce hospital stay, ensure faster recovery, and provide better aesthetic results. Also, technology can also contribute to the surgical field with robotic medicine where it provides greater precision in surgical movements. As the surgeon's manipulations on the console turn into surgical arms, normal hand shake is eliminated, resulting in unprecedented surgical skill. It also allows the surgeon to perform difficult surgical procedures. The surgical tools of the robotic arms can carry out all the movements that the human hand performs with greater skill and precision.

Today, Kinect's technology is used beyond its original goals in medical therapy.

Example 1

The Microsoft Research Department has made many collaborations in a number of areas. At a University of Minnesota, researcher Nikolaos Papanikolopoulos uses Kinect to help diagnose mental disorders in children. Lancaster and Newcastle are universities that collaborate with Microsoft to create virtual views that interact with their real environment.

Example 2

The Japanese company NSK has built a robot dog based on a project of the University of Electro-Communications (UEC), in the hope of serving as a guide for visually impaired people. A Microsoft Kinect Motion Sensor is positioned in the position where the head would normally be, which helps it more easily identify obstacles and steps. His legs have also been improved to move around obstacles and stairs. In addition to Kinect, it also includes sensors that are integrated into cars and warns of obstacles. Researchers are now trying to incorporate voice commands, while the plans for the future include the integration of a GPS.

Example 3

Researchers from the University of the United Kingdom use technology to help patients recovering from a stroke. They have designed a special algorithm that allows therapists to remotely monitor the movements of the hands and fingers of the patients. In this way they can guide them in performing various exercises included in a wider physiotherapy program.

3. Leap Motion Technology

Leap Motion is an Apple product and was developed for the first time in 2008 when one of the founders, David Holz, began developing the software while studying for a Ph.D in mathematics. Frustrated by the limited features of the mouse and keyboard, he developed this application. It's an extremely accurate way to track the physical movement of the hand and the fingers.

Leap Motion had publicly announced its first product, originally called The Leap. The first appearance was on May 21, 2012. The company launched a software development program in October 2012. That's why it gave 12,000 devices to developers who were interested in creating applications for the device.

The Leap Motion implementation team is, Micheal Buckwald Chairman and Chief Executive Officer, David Holz and Tom Kaweski, General Legal Advisor.

Leap Motion has worked with ASUS and in 2013 released high end notebooks. Also in the same year, it announced another deal with Hewlett Packard to integrate its technology into HP computers. In December of the same year, Leap Motion technology was incorporated into eleven HP devices, including laptop keyboards.

Leap Motion has a height of 13 millimeters, a width of 13 millimeters and a weight of 45 grams. The Leap Motion Controller monitors all movements on all ten fingers up to 1/100 th of a millimeter. One hand has 29 bones, 29 joints, 123 links, 48 nerves and 30 arteries. It is the most sensitive of the existing motion control technologies and in this way gives us the ability to program and design very demanding applications with regard to the accuracy of motion.

3.1. Leap Motion Input Devices

The controller can be described as a visual monitoring system based on stereoscopic vision. According to official information, Leap Motion software analyzes the objects seen in a device control field. It recognizes hands, fingers, gestures, and movement. Its field of control is an inverted pyramid in the center of the device. The effective range of the controller extends about 600 millimeters above the device. The controller itself is accessible and scheduling through programming languages (APIs), including programming languages, including C ++ and C #.

Leap Motion uses IR images to illustrate and determine the location of the user's gesture. Leap Motion uses two IR cameras in combination with the three IR LEDs. The image provides settings that contain the brightness values of the sensor and settings that contain the camera calibration map, which can be used to correct lens distortion and other visual flaws in the image data. The image data is provided as a pixel array. The infrared format uses one byte per pixel, which determines the brightness measured for that sensor location. We can display the data in infrared as the gray scale of the image.

3.2. Leap Motion and API

As we discussed in the section above, the Application Programming Interface API refers to the set of functions provided by a programming library to provide communication with the operating system or control program or device. Without allowing access to the code, Leap Motion technology provides us with an API that is the Leap SDK Api. The latest version of Leap Api introduces a new skeletal tracking model that provides additional information on the hands and fingers, as well as improving tracking data.

By modeling a human hand, Leap Motion software can predict and better focus the fingertips. During the detection of the hand there are always five fingers which can be either stretched or not. In addition, fingers can be crossed during their monitoring, so we need to be careful to accurately locate the finger position.

3.2.1. Leap SDK Api Includes

- Right or left hand recognition
- Identify the digits
- Report the position and orientation of each finger bone
- Report factors if a user seeks a hold of a grip
- Report five fingers in each hand

Additionally, the Leap SDK uses classes that represent objects such as hand gestures, hands and fingers.

The Leap Motion system recognizes and records the hands and fingers. The device works with high precision proximity and monitors movements and gestures in distinct positions.

The Leap Motion controller uses optical sensors and infrared light. The sensors are directed along the y - axis upwards when the controller is in the normal operating position and have a field of view of about 150 degrees. The effective area of Leap Motion ranges from about 25 m, 600 mm above the device

3.2.2. Coordinate System

Leap Motion uses a Cartesian coordinate system. Origin is centered on the Leap Motion Controller's top. The x and z axes are in the horizontal plane, with the x-axis parallel to the long side of the device. The y axis is vertical, with positive values rising upwards.

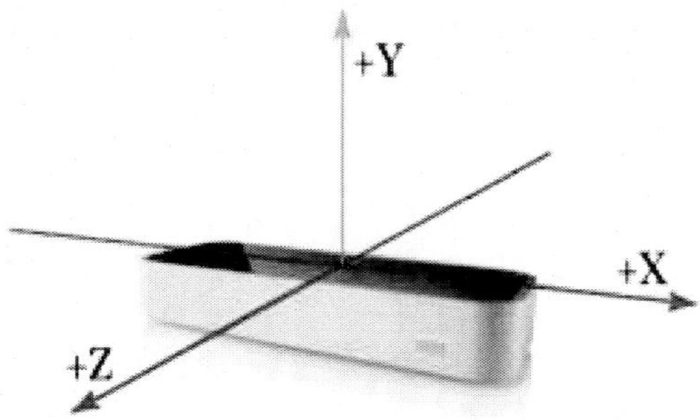

Image 3. Coordinate System Leap Motion.

The Leap Motion Controller provides coordinates of real-world units. That is, if the position of an edge of a finger is given as (x, y, z) = [100,100, -100], these numbers are x = + 10 cm, y = 10 cm, z = -10 cm.

3.2.3. Hand Model on the Leap SDK

The hand model provides information about the identity, position, and other hand features when detecting the gesture.

Leap Motion software provides tracking, even when parts of the hand are not visible. The hand model always provides five finger positions where monitoring is optimal and all fingers are visible. Note that fine finger movements are protected by Leap Motion sensors and are not usually detectable. It is also advisable to keep up to two hands in the Leap Motion field for optimal motion tracking quality.

In this hand model we have two parameters:

- Palm Normal. It is the vector perpendicular to our palm.
- Direction. It is the vector parallel to our palm.

3.2.4. Finger Model Leap SDK

The Leap Motion controller provides information on each finger in one hand. If all or part of the fingers are not visible, the fingerprints are then calculated on the basis of the most recent observations. Fingers are identified by the type name, i.e., thumb, index, middle, and small.

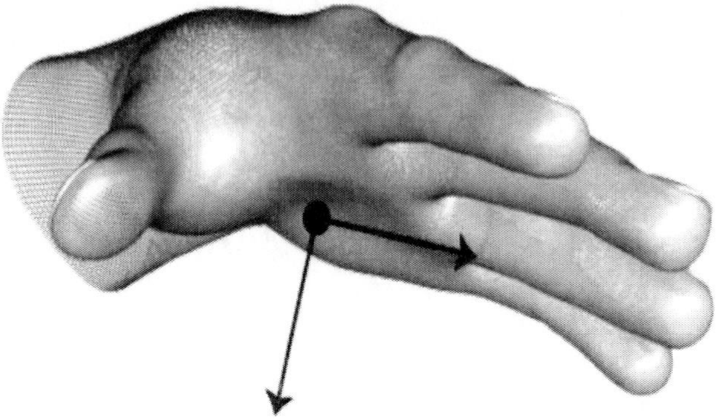

Image 4. Hand Model.

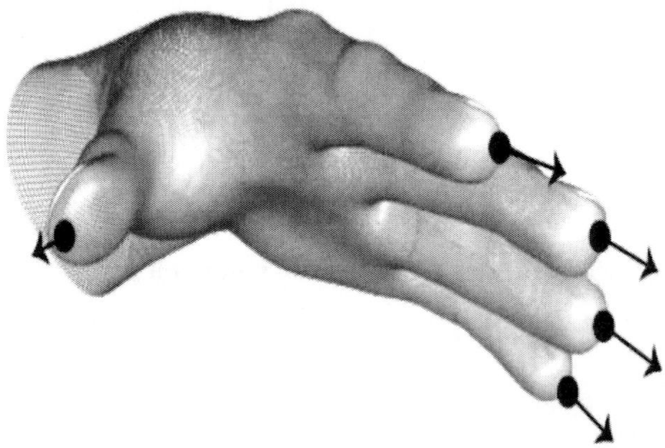

Image 5. Finger Model.

In this finger model we again have two parameters:

- Tip position. It is the vector of the position of our finger on the coordinate axis.
- Direction. It's the direction of our finger.

3.2.5. Bone System

For every finger we have the bone system. Where for each finger we have:

- Metacarpal the bone inside the hand that connects the finger to the wrist (except the thumb).
- Proximal Phalanges the bone at the base of the finger, attached to the palm
- Intermediate Phalanges the middle finger of the finger between the top and the base
- Distal Phalanges the fingertip

In fact, the thumb has fewer bones than the other fingers (no metacarpus). However, for ease of programming, the finger model includes a zero-length metacarpal bone so that the thumb has the same number of bones as the rest of the fingers.

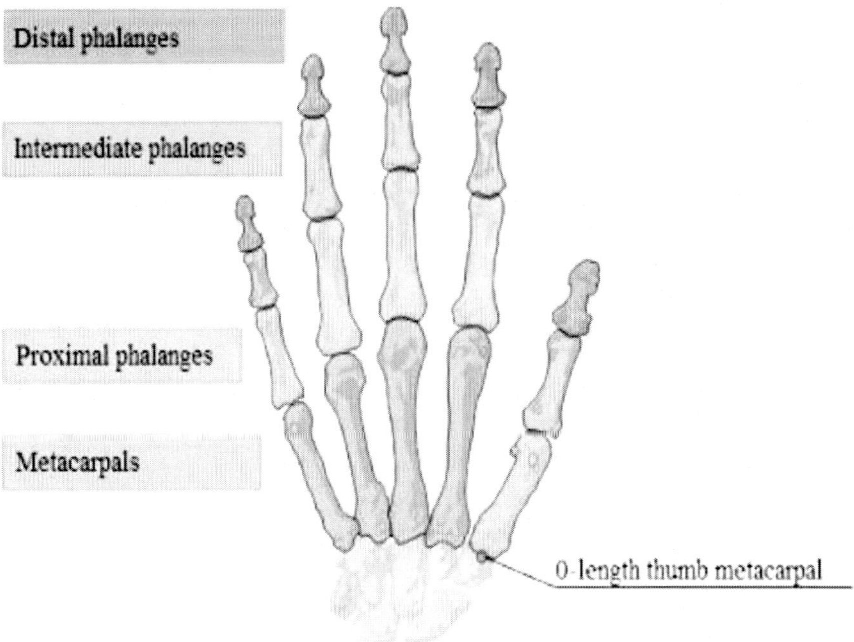

Image 6. Bone System.

3.3. Detecting Gestures Leap Motion

Leap Motion software recognizes some motion patterns as gestures that could indicate an intention or command by the user. These gestures are observed for each finger separately as there are specific types of gestures depending on the position of the direction and the direction of the finger.

To enable the gestures, we must activate the enable Gesture () method wherever there are gesture types. There are four types of gestures in the Leap Motion SDK API.

- *Swipe Gesture*. It is the sharp linear motion that is done in front of the computer screen. This gesture is continuous. We can make a move in any direction. As soon as the motion starts, Leap Motion software will update the progress of this gesture. The gesture will stop as soon as the finger or hand changes direction. Programming the Swipe gesture in the Leap Motion SDK API is the Swipe Gesture.
- *Circle Gesture*. It is the circular movement of the finger in space. This gesture is continuous. The software is updated whenever a move starts and stops when the finger changes direction. In this case, the finger changes once when it deviates from the circle. Schedule the Circle Gesture is the Circle Gesture.
- *Key Tap*. It's a fast downward move like when a user presses a key on the keyboard or a key on the piano. This movement recognizes it as a basic gesture and is distinct in time. Programming the Key Tap gesture is the Key Tap Gesture.
- *Screen Tap*. It's a fast forward movement on the computer screen. This motion recognizes it as a basic move to the screen and is also distinct in time.

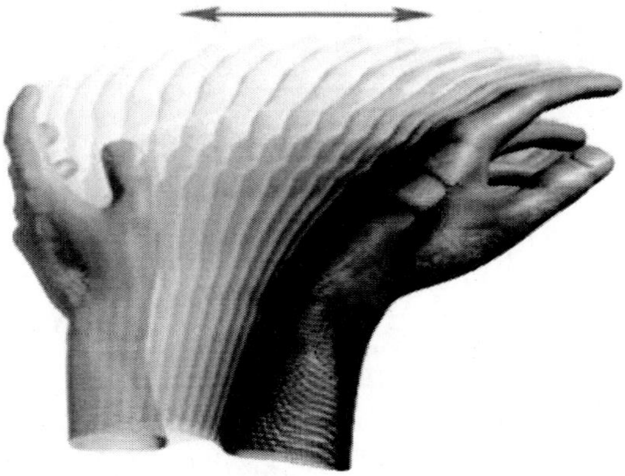

Image 7. Swipe Gesture.

Image 8. Circle Gesture.

Image 9. Key Tap.

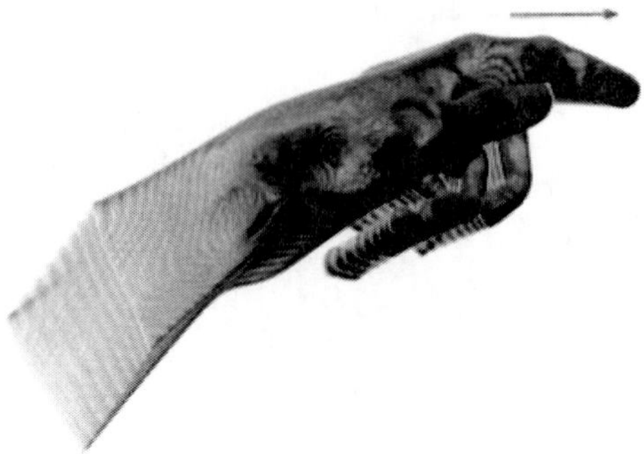

Image 10. Screen Tap.

3.4. App Store Leap Motion

Leap Motion has an App Store called airspace where it sells apps from developers. In November 2013 it was reported that the applications had reached 150.

We can use the Leap Motion App Store to browse and download Leap Motion-enabled applications, web pages, or other products for use with the Leap Motion Controller and our computer. Leap Motion provides the App Store as a service for users to easily discover the features and Leap Motion content. Some of these applications can be offered by Leap Motion, while others may be available from third parties not controlled by Leap Motion.

Leap Motion Computing technology enables us to access applications that allow us to experiment, create and interact using hand movements in a real 3D space.

In the App Store, we can find applications in many categories and disciplines such as medicine and robotics. Many applications are free but others are not because many developers do not provide these applications for free.

To get an app from the Leap Motion App Store, we first need to take a few steps. First we should download the software where these applications are available. When we download the required software, we will be asked to create an App Store where we will import our items. When this stage is completed, we will be able to download and buy whatever application we are interested in. Once we've detected the desired application, what we have to do is click on it and then click on "Get App". At this point, we will be asked again to enter our details and the bank account details.

In order to be able to supply any application we should have the Leap Motion equipment.

As mentioned above, Leap Motion technology has remained at the disposal of developers, giving them a great incentive as well as equipment. Some of the industries that use Leap Motion technology are the Art, Hp, Education and Medical industries.

4. TECHNOLOGY INTERVENTION IN SIGN LANGUAGE

Communication between people requires the use of various means of expression. Man uses different expressions such as speech, gestures, look, facial expression, and body posture. In this way communication between people is achieved either by a combination of these expressions or individually, but for some other people only the gestures and the attitude of the body are sufficient to achieve communication between them. By enabling the user to use everyday communications to interact with the computer, we achieve a more anthropocentric design. The human-to-computer interface can make communication even easier between listening people and people who speak sign language with some who do not know it.

To do this, however, we need the right technology that should be accessible to the average user, such as the microphone and camera that are input devices that, with the proper processing, satisfy some of the above modes of expression, such as speech or facial expression. But to identify the movement of the human body we need different equipment which is more specialized.

In order to be able to supply any application we should have the Leap Motion equipment. As mentioned above, Leap Motion technology has remained at the disposal of developers, giving them a great incentive as well as equipment. Some of the industries that use Leap Motion technology are Art, Hp, Education and Medical industries.

4.1. Community and Deaf

All people have needs. Our everyday lives are full of activities. So we all need to join a group in a community with which we will have the same characteristics and activities. An objective observer can distinguish that the predominant feature of people is their inclusion into groups. The first group is the family, a group without which it would be impossible to survive. When there is no family, then there must be a substitute.

A group and, by extension, a community exists when it fulfills at least four conditions: It satisfies the need for group participation, motivation, firmly built relationships and mutual influence. In the context of the need to participate in groups, a group can be defined as a social unit when it is made up of two or more people who believe they belong to it. So people do not form a group unless they consciously choose it. Two social scientists, Bales and Smith, designate the group in the following way:

"A small group is defined as a number of people interacting and influencing each other, each member being recognized by others as a member and recognizing others as members of the group."

Padden gives the following definition of the deaf community: "the deaf community consists of a group of people living in a region, having common goals defined by its members and struggling to achieve these goals. A community of deaf people can include people who are not deaf, but who support the active purposes of the deaf community and work with the deaf to achieve them." Deaf people themselves do not see themselves as hearing impaired and do not want to have that treatment. Despite the neglect they accept, they try to adapt. They may live in their own society but they are influenced by the wider society. But this also requires the right listeners. Also, as a group, despite their exclusion from the wider society, they have gathered a considerable amount of information and have discovered ways to define and express themselves through traditions, stories, events and everyday social encounters.

Other than reading, sign language is the only natural way of communicating the deaf people. Through it they are served in their everyday lives. In addition to their expression they also use art such as sign poetry, songs in sign, theater and literature. Each country has its own national Sign Language. As we have said above, the particular feature of the sign is that its system of rules is hippocampus. Grammar, morphology and syntax are based on hand movements, body posture and facial expressions, which are integral tools for speech rendering and integrated communication.

The wording of words and meanings is made on two levels:

- The chirp which is the shape of the palm. This in itself, however, does not matter and is not an end.
- Expressions, movement of the body, orientation and the posture of the head and the hands in combination with the chirp are a word in a sentence and the word becomes important.

An important role is also played by the Finger Alphabet that you use in speech primarily to assign the proper names and places. The wording of the concepts is a combination of chirp and body involvement which is determined by the word or concept that we want to formulate.

4.2. Leap Motion

Using Leap Motion technology can identify and translate the Signal Alphabet.

To implement this particular application, it is essential to detect fingerprints, how to capture and how to translate each user's finger movement.

When implementing this application in Leap Motion, we see that it recognizes both hands of the user. However, with the code, it is not so simple to track the left and right hand values because there is also the depth determination value.

At the startup of the crawl, the program first defines the basic hand. Then it checks the condition of each joint of the hand and calculates its position, in this case the right hand. Every time the basic hand makes an action, you update its position. Watching a hand is done by calculating the x, y, z position of the hand in the space.

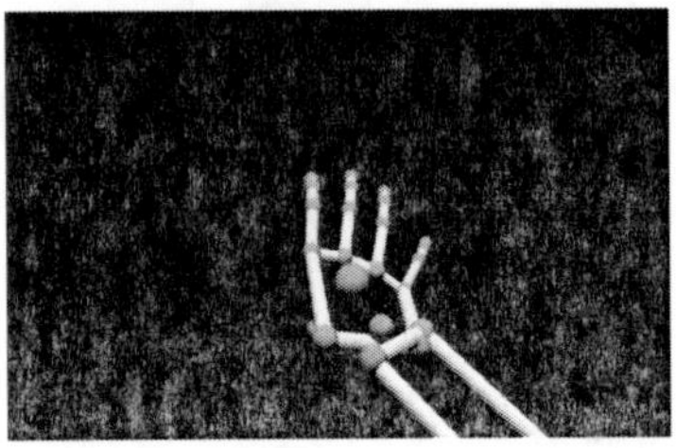

Image 11. Motion Detection with Leap Motion.

5. Intelligent Agent

Intelligent agents are modern Artificial Intelligence systems in which potentially selective and combined methods of representing knowledge and problem solving can be used with technologies presented in the previous chapters. With this in mind, the different basic abstract architectures of intelligent agents are presented. Reference is made to multi-agent systems and their applications are presented.

The emergence of agents, and intelligent agents in particular, in the field of TN and, more generally, in the area of Computer Science, promises radical changes in user-software communication in today's interconnected and networked digital world. Already there is a variety of applications such as search and filtering of information on the internet, providing intelligent help and customer service, as well as checking the correct operation of large factory units.

The term "agent" refers to a person acting on behalf of another person, that is, what we call an agent, may be an alternative agent or an intermediary. More generally, the use of the term dealer is unacceptable, since a dealer simply carries out a number of orders. Instead, an agent is able to fulfill a multitude of goals with minimal user involvement.

It has proved extremely difficult to give a strict definition of the term agent because some of its features have a completely different meaning and weight in the different disciplines investigating the subject. In one, as much as possible, more general an agent is an entity that perceives the environment in which it is located by means of sensors, forms part of its environment, makes thoughts and acts on it by means of action mechanisms (effectors) to achieve target data. The user or some other software entity must have some degree of autonomy (Russel & Norvig, 2009).

A common feature of agents is their autonomy. As autonomous entities, they control their states and behaviors without being externally directed step by step. Other common features are sociability and collaboration with other agents:

- Autonomy: Agents act autonomously without direct intervention by users or other agents, with full control of their actions (self-control) and their internal situation.
- Social ability: Agents interact with users to achieve their goals with other agents through a commonly understood language. Thus communication between agents is accomplished in order to achieve the individual goals of each one and a common goal in cooperation with each other.
- Rationality: It concerns the assumption that an agent will always do the right thing, that is, he will act appropriately to fulfill his goals and not in a way that prevents him from achieving them.

Intelligent agents have additional features regarding their degree of intelligence, such as:

- Reactivity: Refers to the way they perceive the environment and respond to changes within certain timeframes.
- Pro-activeness: Agents do not just respond to changes in their environment but are able to behave appropriately in these changes by defining individual goals (i.e., taking the initiative).

- Knowledge: Concentrated knowledge of how the environment in which each agent operates, appropriately represented, to support decision-making.
- Beliefs: They represent the agent's view of the environment at a given point in time, which view may be incorrect.
- Desires: They relate to the agent's judgment about the future situations of his or her environment, such as, for example, whether a future situation is desirable or not. However, it is not considered whether an agent's desire is feasible or conflicts with another agent.
- Intentions: Intents are a subset of the goals the agent is trying to achieve at that time. Since it is not possible to attain all the objectives simultaneously, a subset is selected based on certain hierarchy criteria.
- Obligations: They concern the agent's obligation to obey a set of rules and act in a more general context in order to achieve the purpose for which they were designed. Adaptivity: The agent adapts to his/her environment (learning ability).

In addition to the features mentioned above, there are additional features that respond to specific categories of agents by offering an "anthropomorphic architecture" of software that allows:

Mobility: It is the ability of an agent to move freely into a physical space or network.

Agent-based cooperation based on:

- Veracity: Agents do not deliberately misinterpret information.
- Benevolence: Each agent strives to achieve their own goals, which are in harmony with the goals of the other system agents

According to the above categorization, intelligent agents are initially divided into two main categories, biological and artificial.

Biological agents use their senses to perceive the world around them, their knowledge, to draw conclusions about it, and the parts of the body to carry out the actions arising from their reasoning.

Artificial agents work in a similar way and are divided into two sub-categories, robotics and computing agents.

5.1. Agents' Environment

So far, the term "environment" has been mentioned several times in which an agent acts. More generally, in a sense environment is the "problem" for which agents are the "solution". Russel & Norvig (2009) categorize agents' environments as follows:

- Fully Observed/Partially Observed: when an agent can receive complete and accurate information through its sensors at any time, the environment is marked as accessible. In a fully accessible environment, an agent is not required to have an internal state for the representation of the environment. On the contrary, in a partially accessible environment, agents do not receive immediate and detailed information about it. Note that the degree of accessibility of the environment also depends on the sensors of each agent. For example, an agent who undertakes to monitor the ambient temperature in which a pump operates and has thermostats only for the water being pumped, the environment is considered to be partially accessible. If another thermostat is added to the metal surrounding the pump, then the agent environment is considered fully accessible.
- Deterministic/Stochastic: If the next state of an environment can be fully determined by its current state and current agent actions, then this environment is called deterministic, otherwise it is characterized as non-deterministic. One general observation is that a fully accessible and deterministic environment facilitates the agent in his actions. Of course, if the environment is partially

accessible, then it is very likely that it is also a non-deterministic environment. This is mainly the case in environments that are complex and make it difficult for the agent to fully understand the current state of his environment.

- Episodic or Sequential: An environment is classified as episodic when divided into discrete episodes. Each episode is characterized by the agent's perception of the environment in which he is at the moment and of his actions within him. Because each episode is independent of previous episode actions, the agent does not look at the effect of his current actions on future episodes. On the contrary, in non-episodic environments it is likely that current actions will have implications for future actions. For example, a weather forecast agent operates in an episodic environment, while an airline ticketing agent operates in a non-episodic environment.
- Static or Dynamic: When an environment can be altered by nature, while an agent acts in it, the environment is characterized as dynamic. When the environment changes, but only because of the agent's actions, it is called semi-dynamic. In all other cases it is characterized as static.
- Discrete/Continuous: This theoretical separation is based primarily on the time conception of the agent through his sensors. In a distinct environment, as in a two-player game played in rounds, the various moves made by each player in his round can be expressed in discrete values (movements). In a continuous environment, such as the operation of a plant, variables such as the movements of automated machines are constantly changing to the unit of time.
- Single Agent/Multiagent: If an agent acts on his own in an environment, the environment is characterized as a unique agent environment, otherwise the environment is multi-agent. The above categorizations ultimately describe the complexity of one environment. The more complex the environment, the more difficult it is to develop a functional agent that acts within it. One important point is that complexity is not a predetermined property of the environment, but depends heavily on the agent's sensors that

interact with it. Two agents of the same function but different sensors acting on the same the environment they perceive differently.

6. Technology Today

From laptops, smart phones, tablets and ... smart clocks. Technology is the central reference point of modern life, culture and reality. Technology can refer to material objects such as machines or utensils, but also to some systems. The first people began their relationship with technology by turning the fossil raw materials into simple tools. Nowadays, there is a tendency for technology to refer only to computer science or symmetrical machinery.

And yet we have cockroaches. Roboroach cockroaches are not like the usual cockroaches. An electronic WiFi device is placed on their belly so you can steer them from a distance. The chip is positioned to excite the special pressure sensors on their bellies and are called beads. With the rays, cockroaches perceive the presence of predators and move accordingly. That's why some researchers (from North Carolina State University) thought cockroaches could become a useful tool in their hands. Of course, it is enough to solve a problem. Have a picture of where they are moving and their traffic is monitored. What is accomplished with other electronic devices such as cameras and software that map space and transmit information to a computer and a Microsoft Kinect system? All this work is aimed at mapping fast-changing areas like a building that has collapsed from an earthquake. In this case, they could help rescue caged people. The original idea, of course, goes a few years back to the MIT Personal Robotics Group. The capabilities offered by Kinect are not limited to gaming, something that has already been noticed since the launch of the first model in 2010. The KinectBot, as they called the first robots, was something among those robotic vacuum cleaners but they functioned like Roboroach. They made three-dimensional maps of the environment and transmitted the information wirelessly to a receiver. The next step was the aerobots, remote-controlled airplanes, that is, with corresponding capabilities.

The development of such a project also contributed to Microsoft's cash prizes to various groups and companies to reward a project with practical applications. A few months ago, Microsoft announced the new version of Xbox One. Immediately, the increased precision in the perception of gestures and movements of the body was detected, even in places with many objects. The new Kinect system detects finger movements, facial expressions, while infrared detectors measure pulse rate.

Kimmetric has developed a particularly commercial application. Many Kinect units are placed in busy places and supermarkets. The data is used to analyze consumer preferences.

On the other hand, IKKOS develops Kinect-based champion training systems to facilitate the learning of specific moves. Kinect detects the movements, compares them to the ideals, and generates feedback on the performance of the athlete. The same system has been applied to the restoration of stroke disabilities.

The most anticipated implementation is the Minority Report. It is now possible to process an object even on the internet without any contact with the keyboard and the mouse. All technology and comfort in our hands. According to the company, thanks to its software, a camera can recognize the user's movements from a distance of up to 5 meters and supports a variety of functions depending on the gestures. For example, with the closing of the punch, an object can be dragged and dropped, while a quick opening and closing of the fingers double clicks. Interestingly, virtual keyboard scripting is of interest, as long as the user is typing around where the letters of a normal keyboard are normal.

6.1. The Evolution of Technology in the Future

Already the development of technology has affected many branches by using topical software. Future changes and the invasion of technology into many rewards are expected in the future, making everyday life a lot easier and safer. It is important to use them for these very purposes.

6.2. Medicine

Medicine is the least computerized science, so rapid changes are expected. The predictions for medicine are not only expected to remotely perform medical interventions and organize medical meetings, which are already possible, but also to complete 3-D body imaging even in a hologram, as well as prescribing and diagnosing by computer and without the intervention of a doctor.

6.3. Control of Thought

Some electronic headers can capture brain signals and then use them to control computers or communicate with other people. A company has developed a computerized system, the BrainGate (Brain Gate), which enables paralyzed people to use their thoughts to handle phones, light switches and other devices. Other systems allow people to type up to 15 words per minute by focusing their minds on the cursor of a computer.

6.4. Artificial Intelligence

Computers can beat top chess players, talk to people, guide robots ... Some scientists believe that one day the machines could replace people altogether. This automation of thought raises one of the most critical questions of our time. Is there a fundamental difference between human intelligence and machine intelligence?

6.5. Robot

A Japanese robot called Asimo can climb stairs and run. Robots "work" as receptionists in offices, waiters and security guards. Japanese and Korean experts are planning in the near future to assign robots for office work, place them in homes as home helpers and even in healthcare.

It is noteworthy that until now people appear particularly "friendly" to robots and can easily become accustomed to their presence as long as they do their jobs. Nurses say that in the near future one in three will have robots in their home. By 2035, state armies will consist exclusively of robots. There are even thoughts about how robots could acquire skills that would make them more human. In research conducted by a British Artist of Artificial Intelligence, it is reported that by 2025 people will fall in love and marry with robots! Already since 2016 in Japan, they have discovered Robots with human skin and capable of having feelings.

6.6. Virtual Reality

One in three people will soon use virtual reality, virtual TV (three-dimensional, with activation and other senses such as touch and smell), and virtual reality web-sites (such as Second Life).

Improving living standards, increasing life expectancy, reducing physical labor, reducing working time, and improving the transfer of knowledge and ideas are some of the beneficial effects of technology.

CONCLUSION

With the rapid development of technology and new applications, we have seen that it is now possible to recognize both movements and gestures. Nowadays, technology is usable in many industries and the main purpose is to facilitate the everyday life of humans. There are many technological tools that can be used as needed. We have seen and analyzed the new technological means and the possibilities that they offer us nowadays. In addition, Microsoft Kinect and Leap Motion were analyzed. We have seen the features and capabilities for each interface instrument. We then compared the two types of interface media. By giving an in-depth analysis and explaining how traffic can be realized and tracked, we are now able to identify which technology is possible for each application.

An example was then taken to translate sign language. To do this, we had to analyze and take into account many different parameters. The most important of these is the culture and characteristics of deaf people. Sign language is not just hand gestures or body movements, it is also the expression of the person and of the person he/she understands. Our differences with deaf people are governed by the way we communicate from the different alphabet we use from the conversation and rules that exist, even for the simplest things we do in our daily routine. Understanding our diversity, we have taken the first step in implementing this application.

In addition, a review was made of today's available applications, generating ideas for new technologies as well as expanding existing ones.

Technology still promises a lot.

REFERENCES

Electronic Media

Editing Blog Mivia, *Flexible Mobile Sending Robot*, [Online], Available at http://blog.mivia.dk/flexible-mission-execution-for-mobile-robots/ [Access Date 11/10/2017].

Editing, G. Antzakas. *The story of the deaf. Faces and events that marked the struggle for autonomy of the deaf community*, [Online], Available in http://neatonamea.blogspot.co.at/2010/02/blog-post_19. html [Access Date 10/10/2017].

Leap Motion editing, *Introducing Skeleton Tracking Model*, [Online], Available at https:// developer.leapmotion.com/documentation/ csharp/ devguide/Intro_Skeleton_AP I.html Copyright © 2017, Leap Motion.

Leap Motion Editing, *Leap Motion*. Available at https://support.leapmotion.com/hc/en-us/sections/205226068-Leap-Motion-App-Store Copyright ©2017, Leap Motion.

Leap Motion Editor, *We're just getting started*., [Online], Available at https://www.leapmotion.com/company Copyright © 2017, Leap Motion, Inc.

Mathematics Editor 2012 Microsoft Kinect, An overview of programming API's. [Online], Available at http:// gmv.cast.uark.edu/ uncategorized/ microsoft-kinect-resourcesprogramming-apis/ Copyright © 2017 - *Geospatial Modeling and Visualization* All logos and trademarks remain the property of their respective owners.

The Guide Dog Robot: Future Mobility Aid for the Blind and Visually Impaired. http://madaportal.org/blogs/guide-dog-robot-future-mobility-aid-blind-and-visually-impaired Copyright © 2017.

Books

Baker, C. & Padden, C. (1978). Focusing on the Non-manual components of American Sign Language. In P. Siple (ed.), *Understanding Language Through Sign Language Research*. London: Academic Press.

Efthimios, Syntihakis. (2012). *Application Development with the use of Microsoft Kinect Sensor*, Technological Applications Degree, Applied Informatics & Multimedia Department, Technological Educational Institute of Crete.

Jarrett, Webb. & James, Ashley. (2012). *Beginning Kinect Programming with the Microsoft Kinect SDK*, Apress, New York, 3-40.

Johnson, D. W. & Johnson, F. P. (1994). *Joining Together: Group Theory and Group Skills*, 5th Edition. Boston: Allyn & Bacon.

Kramer, Jeff, Burrus, Nicolas, Echtler, Florian, Herrera, Castro, Daniel & Parker, Matt. (2012). *Hacking the Kinect*, Apress, New York, 40-42, 50, 55.

Maybury, Mark T. & Wahlster, Wolfgang. *Readings in Intelligent User Interfaces*, 1998, Morgan Kaufmann Publishers.

Padden, C. & Humphries, T. (1988). *Deaf in America. Voices from a Culture, Society and Deaf.* First training package. Special Education/Deaf Unit of the University of Patras.

Padden, C. (1980). The deaf community and the culture of deaf people. In C. Baker and R. Battison (eds.), *Sign Language and the Deaf Community*. Silver Springs, MD: National Association of the Deaf.

In: Gesture Recognition
Editors: G. Coleman and R. Ward ISBN: 978-1-53613-491-9

Chapter 2

FACIAL GESTURE RECOGNITION AND ITS APPLICATIONS

Kornel Bertok and Attila Fazekas*
Faculty of Informatics, University of Debrecen,
Debrecen, Hungary

ABSTRACT

Computer based facial gesture recognition became a field of intense interest in human-computer interactions recently. The aim of this field of science is to translate several facial information into a human-like and human-interpretable description in order to communicate with computers in a more natural way. The domain of facial gesture recognition problems can be defined easily, however the algorithms should work beside various facial positions, orientations and appearances that can result a considerable obstacle in the implementation. The first step of facial gesture recognition is the determination of those atomics that are relevant in production of the facial gestures themselves. Such atomics are the location of the face; the position of several facial feature points; the spatial position and orientation of the face or head; the changes in location or appearance taking place in time. This chapter presents our approach for face detection and tracking, user identification, facial feature

---

* Corresponding Author Email: attila.fazekas@inf.unideb.hu.

extraction and head pose estimation as the low-level representation of facial gesture atomics. At a higher level, we give an approach for a movement based facial gestures recognition and we demonstrate our results through practical approaches as some applications of facial gesture recognition.

Keywords: face detection, facial gesture recognition, human-computer interaction

INTRODUCTION

Nowadays, information technology has a significant effect on our everyday life. The role of information processing and content handling tends to be more and more determinative as different electronic smart devices are becoming a part of daily life. There is an instinctive expectation regarding the way of using these devices, such as communicating with them in a manner which is more natural and efficient than it used to be. Even today, a significant amount of studies and solutions has emerged for analyzing the information that has been transmitted by human agents to computers. A particular field of science has been formed recently in order that communication with computers can be made as evident as possible for the human party. This field of science is called *Human-Computer Interactions* (HCI), and it is sometimes also referred to as *Human-Machine Interactions* (HMI). HCI is not a new branch of science as it was introduced in the 1980s, and initially it was used to improve the usage of computers (in terms of how easy it is to learn with them) by combining cognitive and computer sciences. Since then, a significant amount of progress has taken place mostly by incorporating new fields of sciences, and it is also obvious that the relevance of HCI will be among the most promising and forward-looking IT trends in the future.

Together with user experience, HCI is getting more and more emphasized as it serves humans to communicate with computers in a novel and more natural way – not only via well-known input devices (e.g., keyboards or touchscreens), or graphical user interfaces. HCI focuses on interfaces between humans and computers, and in this way it affects and evolves the quality of the way of interactions. At the end of the evolution, there are HCI interfaces that are focused on multimodal and adaptive nature of their own in order to make human-computer communication as axiomatic and evident as human-human communication is. For instance, simple webcams can be used for feeding applications with human behavioral or expressional factors back to computers. Such information can further be used for adapting the behaviour of a system. Thus computers will be able to respond in such a cognitive way as it would be done by humans.

In HCI, human and machine parties can be considered to be equal as they are taken into account at the same time – with the same significance. However, it is obvious that the focus is always on the end user's satisfaction. HCI has a certainly multidisciplinary nature, consequently it needs knowledge of both human (e.g., communication theory, cognitive sciences or linguistics) and machine aspects (e.g., computer sciences or engineering). Interactions can be more reflective and realistic due to this multidimensional nature and the process of how humans interact with computers evolves continuously with the development of technology. The forces which are shaping the nature of future computing systems have a predictable effect on HCI. For instance, decreasing hardware costs result in faster and more portable systems where the fusion of different fields is getting stronger and stronger. Nowadays the results are not only academically-focused, since lots of them have already emerged in industry, i.e., developers and designers are involved in manufacturing products which use the latest results of HCI in a web service or in a smartphone application.

This study focuses on a subset of HCI: *facial gesture recognition* in the field of computer vision. Gesture recognition is often referred to as *human activity recognition* (HAR) within the field of HCI. Gesture recognition involves interpreting and recognizing human gestures via mathematical models and algorithms. These are sometimes just simple decision functions on primitive feature vectors, or they are complex machine learning algorithms with the ability of making decisions without being explicitly implemented or formulated. A gesture can be performed by the motion of a body part – e.g., head nodding – or it can be a given state of the configuration of some body parts – e.g., a finger of a hand is pointing to the right. A gesture is most often made by a hand or head. This study only focuses on facial gestures which are performed by the head. Systems that are able to deal with facial gestures have the ability to communicate them without any physical interaction, in other words, with the use of gesture recognition there is no need for a keyboard or touchscreen as an input device.

Gesture recognition is commonly used during the design and development of a *perceptual user interface* (PUI). PUI enables an end user to interact with a computer more generally without having any physical contact during communication. The main goal of PUI is to enhance HCI for example by understanding head movements or voice commands. PUI can be built upon as a top layer of an underlying, existing application since gestures are often used as input commands. In this way, gesture control can be redundant for traditional control devices, and later on it can substitute them by continuous improvements and end users' acceptance. For instance, a couple of years ago gesture recognition was barely used in industry, but today there are smartphones which can be unlocked by a user's face, and even more functionalities of touchscreens can be replaced by touchless user interfaces in the future.

FACIAL GESTURE RECOGNITION PROBLEM

As it has been discussed above, facial gesture recognition is essential in communication with computers. Gesture recognition can be referred to as human activity recognition (HAR) in the field of HCI and hereinafter we will term it as HAR as well. HAR, however, does not simply equal gesture recognition, it is based on the definition of interactions and includes the recognition of any kind of actions or configurations performed by human end-users using a series of observations about the human party. HAR appears as a standalone layer within communication, and it aims to deliver a new interface during HCI which is more natural than the way in which computers communicate nowadays (i.e., by controlling an application with pre-defined head movements). The input set of HAR contains several attributes of the human party. These attributes can even be measured and indexed over time dimension when HAR focuses on the whole ongoing facial gesture instead of the resulting body configuration of the action. For completeness, the HAR problem is usually defined over a time axis while the second one is just a subset of this one [1]:

Definition 1 (HAR problem (HARP)): Given a set $S = \{S_0, \ldots, S_{k-1}\}$, of k input time series together with a set $L = \{L_0, \ldots, L_{l-1}\}$ of l output labels. Each $S_i \in S$ is from a particular measured attribute of the user, and all of them are defined within a time interval $I = [t_\alpha, t_\omega]$. Furthermore, each label $L_j \in L$ represents the activity (e.g., head shaking or nodding) performed during a given interval $I_k \subseteq I$. The goal of HAR is to find a temporal partition $\langle I_0, \ldots, I_{r-1}\rangle$ of I based on the data of S and assign a label $L_j \in L$ to each interval I_k. It implies that each I_k is consecutive, non-empty, non-overlapping, such as $\bigcup_{k=0}^{k=r-1} I_k = I$. Every HAR problem can be given as an ordered triple $HARP = (S, I, L)$, comprising an input set of measured attributes S, an output set of time intervals I together with an output set of labels L.

In this book chapter gestures are performed by a user's head, therefore some features – such as the elements of the attribute set – need to be extracted from the head or face in order to solve the HAR problem. In the following, we will attempt to introduce a new approach with the ability of recognizing complex head movements as human activities. The spatio-temporal representation of head movements starts with the localization of the head or face itself. For portability and comfortability reasons only one webcam is taken into consideration as an observer of the human party. In other words, there is no need for expensive sensors, complicated calibrational procedures and nothing has to be hung onto the user.

STEPS OF THE PREPROCESSING

The usage of simple webcams during HAR makes the approach widely available, however, users perform gestures in 3-D space. We will demonstrate that this issue can be overcome by the 2-D projection of a generic 3-D head model, consequently the attribute space of the HAR problem can be defined in 3-D space. For this reason, several 2-D landmarks (feature points, e.g., corners of eyes, or nose tip) need to be determined on the face. The process starts with the localization of the user's face over the elements of an image sequence.

Face Detection

The face is detected by the well-known algorithm of Viola and Jones [2], which became a de-facto standard for object detection in the past decade. The goal is to distinguish faces (positives) from non-faces (negatives). The Viola and Jones algorithm provides a high true-positive rate and a low false-positive rate at the same time with relatively low computing costs. The algorithm is built around the following three main concepts: a new *image representation* (originally integral images); using variants of the *AdaBoost learning algorithm* in order to select the best features and to train classifiers using only them; using a *cascade architecture* of several weak classifiers in order to create a final strong classifier.

For image representation, originally the Haar-like features were proposed. A Haar-like feature operates with neighboring rectangular regions with different weights at a specific location in a detection window, and concerns the sum of pixels within all regions. Each feature assigns a real number to the current window by calculating the weighted sum between the sums of the regions. This weighted sum describes the subsection at a specific location; therefore, it can used for categorizing a detection window. The whole detection window can be described with a small subset of the features, and the decision about positivity or negativity can be made beside high accuracy. For example, considering a face database, it is obvious that the region of an eye is darker than its surrounding region and a proper feature can be chosen for describing this region of the face. An advantage of the Haar-like features is that they can be generated quickly and efficiently by using a *summed-area table* that is referred to as an integral image in the image processing domain. Another advantage of feature description is that the representation becomes more robust regarding changes or noises in the local appearance because it deals with broader regions instead of single pixels.

Face Tracking

The Viola and Jones algorithm allows us to detect faces in a relatively clean and fast way; however, it does not fulfill the criteria of real-time operation on video streams that have higher resolution than VGA. Furthermore, the detector also fails in such cases when a user turns or tilts his/her head. This limitation comes from the way of training the model for detection since the positive dataset contains only frontal faces in order to reach the highest accuracy. In practice, face detection is always combined with a face tracking method: the face detector is not allowed to run on every frame, it is applied only with a specified frequency (i.e., on every 15th milliseconds) and then the face is tracked in the meantime.

The reason why tracking algorithms are faster than object detection is simple: a lot of information (e.g., location, direction, motion and appearance) becomes available about the object at the moment when it is detected on a frame. Thus, in the next frame, this extra knowledge can be used to predict the next location of the object. A good tracking algorithm considers all available knowledge about the object, while the detector needs to work in an unknown environment. Nevertheless, tracking has a price since low tracking errors between the consecutive frames might quickly accumulate a high error that might be manifested in the following phenomenon: the bounding box of the target that is being tracked starts to drift slowly away from the real position of the object itself. This is the reason why the detector should be applied regularly on the frames, i.e., the tracking algorithms should be initialized repeatedly with the output of object detection.

The definition of tracking sounds quite straightforward, however, in computer vision the term of tracking covers a wide area (e.g., dense or sparse optical flow, meanshift or camshift). The discussion of different tracking algorithms does not fit in the scope of the current book chapter, but fortunately, the conditions during performing gestures allow us to use a very simple tracking approach. As the user sits in front of the screen and the camera, his/her face can be seen as frontal or near-frontal to the device, therefore the appearance of the face does not change much in time and in space. A simple appearance based tracking algorithm can predict the approximation for the object's location accurately. The tracker takes a template (according to the output of face detection) as an input image patch from the previous frame and returns a location with a score over the current frame. The score is a probability that indicates the confidence of tracking. The approximation of a new location is performed by the estimation of normalized cross correlation between the template and the input image at several locations – where the normalization supports us to reduce the effect of different conditions. If there is a correlation between the template and the input image, the template is updated from its new location, and tracking is repeated until a new hit comes from the detector.

User Identification

Another advantage of using tracking algorithms is that those identities can be attached to the detected objects. While the output of face detection is just a set of rectangles, the tracking algorithm establishes connection between the rectangles and the consecutive frames. Some kind of metadata can be assigned to the users during the tracking procedure, such as the time of the last detection, the current bounding box and the appearance of the face, etc. Some metadata is visualized in Figure 1.

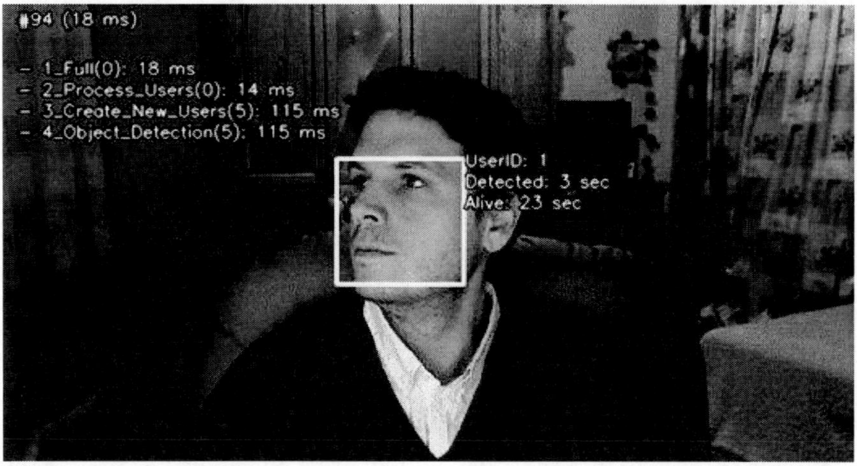

Figure 1. Visual representation of face detection, tracking and identification. While the runtime of the last detection takes took ms, tracking and identification takes 15-20 ms of runtime between two detections.

It can be seen that the current user is present for 23 seconds and the last detection was performed 3 seconds ago. The time complexity of face detection can be ten times higher than tracking and identification. The metadata can be estimated and recorded for the complete lifetime of interactions in order to make more complex decisions for further processing steps. The steps of identification are described below:

- New user identities can be created only by face detection:
  - If a rectangle from the face detection overlaps more than 80% with one of the bounding boxes of a tracked user, an existing identity is found and the corresponding metadata is updated with the new detection,
  - Otherwise, a new user identity is created based on the detection.
- Existing user identities are continuously tracked over the incoming image sequence:
  - If tracking is successful, the user identity is considered to be present,
  - Otherwise, the identity with all of its metadata is deleted as it cannot be tracked any more,

- As a final clause, identities that do not receive any object detection for 10 seconds are deleted as well. More than 10 seconds of tracking without any object detection can accumulate a very high error.

Facial Feature Extraction

Users can perform head movements in 3-D space, thus gestures should be recognized in the same space as well. All the necessary information – attributes of the HAR problem – in 3-D space can be provided by a 2-D projection of a generic 3-D head model. For this reason, some feature points of a face's geometry need to be determined first. In this chapter, a *feature-based approach* will be described that takes the advantage of the geometry of facial features (i.e., the nose tip or the corners of the eyes) and uses a so-called deformable model in order to approximate the 2-D locations of facial features as much as possible.

There are several statistical models of the shape of an object, which – among others – rely on 2-D landmark points and iteratively deform the shape along the landmarks to fit the shape over an object candidate in a new image. The simplest family of statistical models is called *Active Shape Models* (ASMs) [3, 4]. ASM needs some prior information about the objects' shape before fitting itself over a new image and this information is determined during the training phase. ASM focuses on the shape itself, which is by definition the external boundary of an object and furthermore any shape can be represented by its landmarks[3]. Let s denote an arbitrary shape:

$$s = \{p_i \in \mathbb{R}^n : i = 1 \dots N\}, \tag{1}$$

where the final contour can be given by the concatenation of each landmark p_i of s. As our domain is the set of several 2-D images as planar

[3] The object can be considered to be a face and the landmarks are identical to facial feature points in our case.

objects therefore $n = 2$ in our case. Thus, each $p_i = (x_i, y_i)$ and any $s \in \mathbb{R}^{2N}$ shape is represented as a vector with $2N$ components:

$$s = (x_1 \dots x_N, y_1 \dots y_N)^T. \tag{2}$$

Model construction starts with a training phase including an annotated database. The database contains a set of shapes of several faces and at the very first step, ASM aligns them in a common coordinate system in order to determine a mean shape. This is performed by *Generalized Procrustes Analysis* (GPA), which optimally aligns a set of objects instead of aligning them over a freely chosen shape [5]. In other words, GPA minimizes the least squared error between the corresponding landmarks of different shapes. The term "alignment" means the translation, rotation and uniform scaling of an object. The consideration behind the alignments is to obtain a similar arrangement (in placement and size) among the different shapes in order to specify a mean shape that characterizes the complete database. Shapes in the common coordinate system can be considered to be the density function of a random variable in 2-D. It is obvious that the dimensionality of the shapes ($2N$ with N landmarks) is so high that it does not let the training and fitting be achievable in an efficient way. *Principal Component Analysis* (PCA) is used in order to reduce the complexity of the statistical model. The statistical model of the shape can be defined as follows:

$$s \approx \bar{s} + \Phi b, \tag{3}$$

where $\bar{s}$ is the mean shape estimated by GPA, matrix $\Phi \in \mathbb{R}^{2N \times t}$ contains the eigenvectors that belong to the largest eigenvalues (t), furthermore column vector $b \in \mathbb{R}^t$ is the scale factor of the principal components. The latter can be referred to as the parameter set of the deformable model – the mean shape can be deformed by varying vector b (see Figure 2).

Figure 2. Varying column vector b results in slightly different shapes from mean shape $\bar{s}$.

The statistical shape model of ASM is often referred to as a *Point Distribution Model* (PDM). PDM guarantees that a generated shape s cannot have an arbitrary layout; the generated shapes will be similar to the shapes of the training database. Different kinds of ASMs differ only in the strategy of fitting PDM over an input image. The accuracy of fitting is fundamentally determined by the accuracy of face detection and tracking as the PDM is stretched over the face in the first step. Further steps are the minimization of a cost function that depends on a $b \in \mathbb{R}^t$ parameter vector; a $T = [T_X\ T_Y]$ translation; an $R(\Theta)$ rotation; and an S uniform scaling. The fitting approach is built around the property of the PDM deformability and it iteratively applies some affine transformations until it converges (see Figure 3).

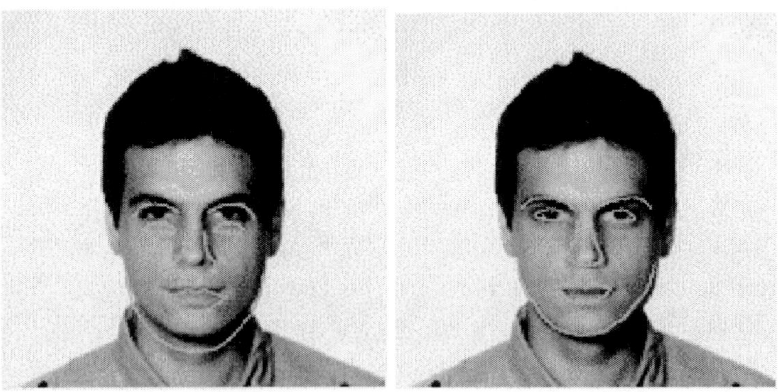

Figure 3. The start-, and end point of the model fitting approach. The image on the *left side* indicates the starting position of the model, where PDM is stretched over the bounding box of a face detector. The image on the *right side* demonstrates the state when convergence is reached.

Head Pose Estimation

In computer vision the combination of an object's position and orientation is often referred to as *pose*. Our goal is to estimate gestures in 3-D space in functions of several 3-D positions and orientations of the head; therefore, the accurate knowledge of the head pose is essential. Deformable models in themselves can also be used for this reason like in [6, 7]. Such approaches take the advantage of the geometry of several facial features. In this chapter, a similar approach is described which was also outlined by us in [8, 9].

Head pose can be determined by the solution of a *Perspective n-Point problem* (PnP problem), thus it can be estimated based on several 2-D and 3-D point correspondences of facial features. 2-D feature points are the results of ASM, thus they are defined on the 2-D image plane of the camera coordinate system: the landmarks $(x_i, y_i), i = 1 \ldots N$ of shapes $s \in \mathbb{R}^{2N}$. 2-D landmarks will be indicated with an upper index C further on, as the computation needs the correspondent 3-D feature points as well. The 3-D model points are provided by sampling a generic 3-D head model according to the 2-D landmarks. Thus, our 3-D points are defined in a generic model coordinate system, so they will be upper-indexed with M further on. The relation between the 2-D landmarks and the 3-D model points can be expressed as follows: a point $p_i = \left(x_i^C, y_i^C\right)$ is the projection of a 3-D model point $P_i = \left(x_i^M, y_i^M, z_i^M\right)$ as it can be seen in Figure 4.

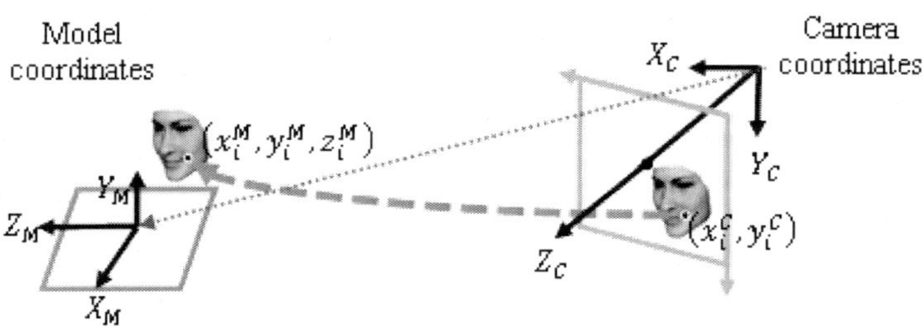

Figure 4. Coordinate systems of head pose estimation. Head pose is essentially the 3-D position and 3-D orientation of the model coordinate system relative to the camera coordinate system.

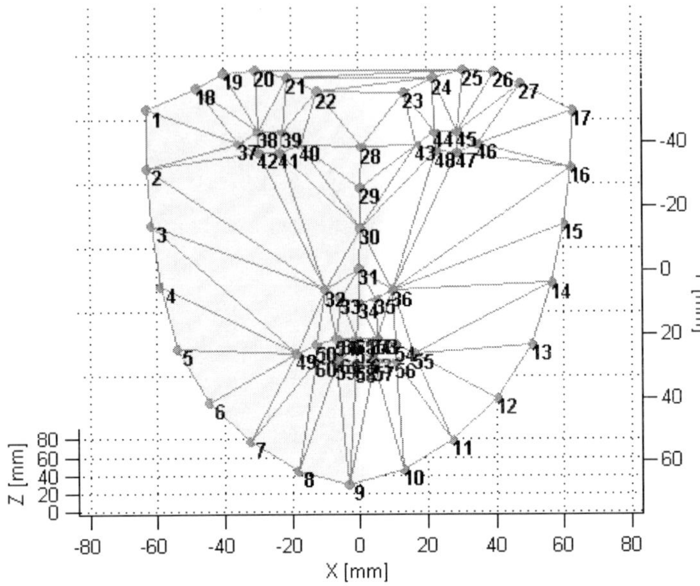

Figure 5. The 3-D model of the face. The 3-D red points belong to the 2-D landmarks of ASM.

The 3-D model points are obtained by a stereo face database [15] (see Figure 5). The depth map that is created from the stereo images has accuracy of 0.32 mm along each axis and this can be considered high enough to estimate the 6 DoF and recognize the gestures based on it later on.

Most of the PnP solutions are based on three (or more) point pair correspondences, e.g., if there are $n = 3$ point pairs, the problem is referred to as a *P3P problem* which is the simplest case. A P3P problem is based on the vertices of a triangle in 3-D space and its 2-D planar projections and provides at least eight different solutions for the triangle's pose [10][4]. Nevertheless, the PnP problem can have a unique solution by using four points, thus the *P4P problem* might yield unambiguous results under several conditions. There are two cases: on the one hand, if the four points are located in a common plane of 3-D space, a problem might have a unique solution; otherwise it might have two different solutions. There

[4] Four solutions can be filtered out simply as they are behind the camera.

are multiple ways and popular approaches in the literature for solving a PnP problem, some of them are non-iterative that provide the analytical solution of the problem. Such a method is EPnP which solves the problem in O(n) time [11]; or RPnP which needs less than five correspondences to find the optimal solution in O(n) time [12]. On the other hand, there are methods that are approximating the exact solution iteratively, e.g., LHS which can be considered to be the best iterative solution of the problem [13]. We have chosen_another iterative P4P approach based on our previous experience [8] and [9]: *Pose from Orthography and Scaling with ITerations* (POSIT) [30]. The head pose with relation to the world coordinate system is estimated and provided by POSIT as a rotation matrix R and translation vector t in 3-D space. The starting point of the solution is the equation of the pinhole camera model:

$$p_i = A[R|t]P_i, \tag{4}$$

where $A \in \mathbb{R}^{3\times 4}$ projection or camera matrix contains *intrinsic parameters* (i.e., focal lengths and principal point) and a 3-D point in homogeneous coordinates of camera coordinate system can be projected onto the 2-D image plane by this matrix. The camera matrix has such a good property that it does not depend on the scene viewed, thus it should be estimated only once (e.g., with a chessboard-based calibration). The elements of the joint rotation-translation $[R|t]$ matrix are the *extrinsic parameters* of the pinhole camera. The 3-D points of the world coordinate system can be transformed to a 3-D camera coordinate system by these rotations and translations. The extrinsics depend on the scene viewed and mean the object's pose. The pose expressed by rotation R and translation t to the camera coordinate system can be estimated with POSIT when the model coordinate system is chosen as the world coordinate system. Thus, the extrinsics bring the 3-D points from the model coordinate system to the 3-D camera coordinate system and then projection to the image plane is done by the intrinsics.

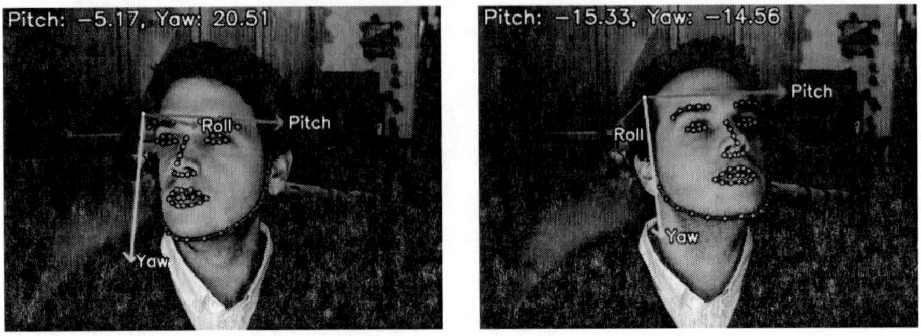

Figure 6. Results of the head pose estimation based on POSIT. Instead of the shape of ASM, the pre-defined 3-D was projected to the image plane and displayed as the shape of the face. The distance to the camera is color coded by red-green transitions.

We will not describe how POSIT operates in detail, but it only needs at least four non-coplanar points in the model coordinate system (this is guaranteed as the face is not a planar object), and then it iteratively approximates and refines the perspective projection of the model points by scaled orthographic projection. In each iteration, the approach solves a linear system of equations where the results are an approximation of the head pose and the approximation is used as an input of the next iteration to refine the approximated head pose until it converges to the final one. Some results of the head pose estimation can be seen in Figure 6.

Representation of Facial Gestures

There have already been several studies where the head pose is used to define and recognize a few action primitives, like in [15, 16, 17, 18]. Obviously, these primitives do not allow us to recognize human activities that are more complex than performing a looking right movement with the head. A proper spatiotemporal representation of head movements is essential in order to recognize complex actions. Our representation is based on facial features and derived pose that have already been described above. In the following, head movements will be considered as time series which are performed over an approximately three or five-second time interval, but there are no strict limitations. Undoubtedly, different head movements are performed in different ways or tempos – even if they are performed intentionally and by the same user –, thus head movements will vary in time or in speed and the corresponding time series will be different from each other. Consequently, the linear alignment is not possible between two different time series; there is a need for a non-linear one in order that the degree of similarity can be estimated. In this section, we will show how the attribute set of the time series can be built up; how head movements can be located in time dimension; and finally, how recognition can be put into practice.

Spatial Representation

Spatial representation is defined by the 6 DoF head pose over consecutive frames. We note here that the environment is fixed as the camera is attached to the screen and does not change its location while the user is performing head movements. Furthermore, we also assume that users sit in front of the screen, hence their location in the world can be considered to be permanent as well. The degree of freedoms of the 6 DoF head pose can only be limited into orientations, therefore the translation vector t can be considered to be zero. It is obvious that the rotation around the (roll) axis Z does not have an important role since the human head is not able to perform roll-directional movements, but we can leave it among the degree of freedoms for simplicity. Accordingly, feature space $\mathcal{F}$ of the attributes is derived only from the orientations around axes X (pitch), Y (yaw) and Z (roll). Let us rotate the unit vector of the model reference frame $\underline{k} = (0,0,1)$ by the orientation of the current head pose, and denote the resulted vector with $\underline{k}_i$ on the ith frame. An $a_i \in \mathcal{F}$ attribute – an observation on the ith frame – of the HAR problem can be defined as:

$$a_i = \underline{k}_i - \underline{k}_{i-1}. \tag{5}$$

Thus, attribute a_i is defined as the difference of the current and the previous rotated vectors and the normalized vector $\underline{k}_i$ can be considered as the direction vector of the head. Hence, attribute a_i encodes the change in the orientation during performing the head movement frame by frame. The norm of vector a_i is close to zero if the head is not really moving, and it has a high value if the movement is intensive. Let us define head movement $m \in \mathcal{M}$ based on attributes $a_i \in \mathcal{F}$. First, let τ be the timestamp of the first observation of a movement and n the number of observations of the same movement. Our observations can be written as $a = (a_\tau, a_{\tau+1}, \dots, a_{\tau+n})$ time series, where time series $a \in S$ is an ordered n-tuple of the HAR problem and can be considered as a sample of a probability distribution. Finally, our head movements $m \in \mathcal{M}$ are defined by the composition of label $l \in L$ (e.g., "head shaking" or "nodding") and time series $a \in S$ created from the observations:

$$m = (l, a_\tau, a_{\tau+1}, \dots, a_{\tau+n}) = (l, a). \tag{6}$$

Thus, the recognition problem of an unknown head movement can be defined as the prediction of the unknown label $l \in L$ based on known attributes $a_i \in \mathcal{F}$. It is recommended to shift all the observations in the time series by a_τ in order to make them independent of the start position, thus the definition of head movements is slightly modified to:

$$m = (l, 0, a_{\tau+1} - a_\tau, \dots, a_{\tau+n} - a_\tau) = (l, a'). \tag{7}$$

Figure 7 below shows an example of the visual representation of attributes $a_i \in \mathcal{F}$ (for a random head movement). The size of a_i is propotional to the intensity of the movement as it is not normalized. Longer arrows around nose position represent more intense movements.

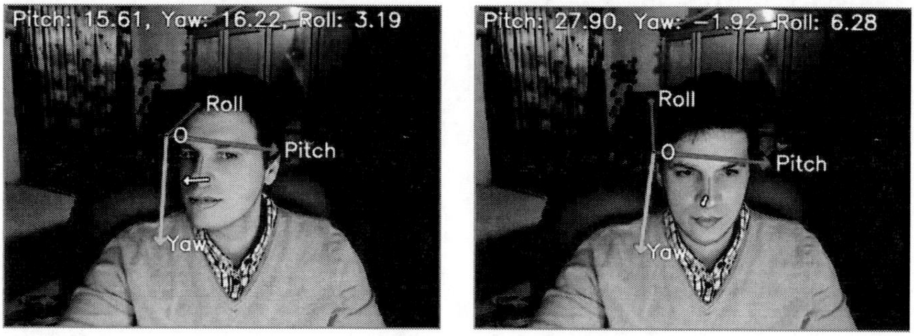

Figure 7. The visual representation of two head movements. The *white arrows* around the nose represent attribute vectors $a_i \in \mathcal{F}$. Their directions correspond to the trajectory of the movement, and their lengths are proportional to the intensity of the movement.

Temporal Representation

Spatial representation is given above, however, temporal representation is not. The temporal representation of head movements means the localization of their starting and ending time. Thus, this representation regarding the HAR problem is the temporal partition of the time interval of the movements I based on data S. The following state-machine can be defined in order to partitionate time interval $I = [\tau_\alpha, \tau_\omega]$ into consecutive, non-empty and non-overlapping time intervals of different head movements. The machine:

- goes to *moving* state: when it is in *non-moving* state, and the norm of a_i goes above a predefined threshold value,
- remains in *moving* state: until the norm of a_i is above a predefined threshold value,
- goes to *ended* state: when it is in *moving* state, and norm of a_i goes below the predefined threshold value,
- goes and remains is *non-moving* state: when it is in *ended* state.

It is obvious that the movements are represented between the moments when the state-machine goes to *moving* state and the moment when it goes to *ended* state. The collection of attributes $a_i \in \mathcal{F}$ must be started when the movement is started, and recognition based on these attributes can be activated when the temporal localization has ended.

FACIAL GESTURE RECOGNITION

The spatiotemporal representation of head movements has already been given above. As it has been mentioned, the time series of different movements will be different from each other – even if they belong to the same kind of movement performed by the same user. Thus, the recognition of head movements needs a non-linear alignment between an unknown and one or more previously known head movements. This non-linear alignment is performed by the algorithm of *Dynamic Time Warping* (DTW), see in [21, 22]. The same kind of method for the recognition of head movements was previously described by us in [9, 20], therefore in this section we will only give its short explanation. DTW is a generative model of joint distribution $p(a, l)$ for head movement $m \in \mathcal{M}$, where $a \in S$ is the time series attributes, and $l \in L$ is the label of the movement (e.g., "nodding"). The goal is to predict $l \in L$ based on time series $a \in S$ when it is unkown. Let us have two head movements: one where the corresponding label is unknown and another where the label is known. Let us refer to the time series of the movement where the label is unknown as *test time series,* and where the label is known as *reference time series*. DTW transforms the time axis of the test time series in such a way that it optimally maps the test time series onto the whole or a part of the reference one. This transformation gives the result of the optimal (least cumulative distortion or distance) alignment between the pair of time series. The optimal alignment is computed by a warping function which considers point-by-point correspondences. DTW also provides a distance-like quantity between a pair of time series that is called DTW distance – it is a semimetric as it satisfies *positivity*, *positive definiteness*, and *symmetry*, but not necessarily *triangle inequality*. Let a pair of time series be given by their attribute set:

$$\begin{aligned} X &:= (x_1, x_2, \dots, x_N) \\ Y &:= (y_1, y_2, \dots, y_M)\text{'} \end{aligned} \tag{8}$$

where time series $X, Y \in S$ have attributes $x_i, y_j \in \mathcal{F}, i = 1 \dots N, j = 1 \dots M$. For clarity, index $i \in [1{:}N]$ will be used for X and $j \in [1{:}M]$ for Y further on.

DTW uses $c: \mathcal{F} \times \mathcal{F} \to \mathbb{R}_{\geq 0}$ cost function (e.g., Euclidean distance) in order to compare attributes x_i and y_j and creates a cost matrix $C \in \mathbb{R}^{N \times M}$ between time series X and Y:

$$C(i,j) = c(x_i, y_j) \geq 0. \tag{9}$$

The alignment between X and Y can be estimated by matrix C, however, the time series can be aligned along multiple paths in C. The path that has the lowest cost is called the *optimal alignment* between time series, and this can be determined by solving an optimization problem according to cost function c. *Warping function* $w(t)$ is used in order to determine the optimal alignment. The warping function establishes the connection between the time indeces of the attributes respectively in such a way that it maps time series X and Y into a common and normalized time axis. Parameter $t \in [1{:}T]$ is the range of this common axis and T is the length of the warped time series.

The averaged accumulated distortion $d_w(X, Y)$ between time series X and Y can be estimated by cost matrix C, warping function $w(t)$ and some other weighting coefficients and normalizing constants. The optimal warping function has the property of minimizing distortion $d_w(X, Y)$:

$$D(X, Y) = \min_{w} d_w(X, Y). \tag{10}$$

The solution for the optimization problem in the equation above is not in the scope of the current study, but we note that it can be solved with time complexity $O(N \cdot M)$ by adding some constraints to the properties of the optimal warping function [23]. Figure 8 shows an example alignment between time series A and B of two head movements. The movements were performed by two different users who had to draw a letter k by their heads. The path along the major axis illustrates the optimal warping path over the cost function. Time series A and B can be considered quite similar as the optimal warping path passes in the neighborhood of the main diagonal of the cost matrix.

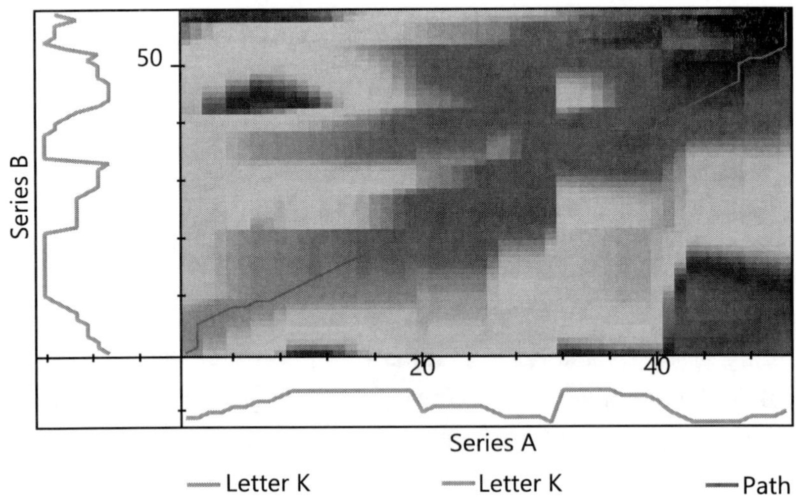

Figure 8. Finding the optimal alignment between time series A and B. The time series are denoted by orange and green functions along the axes. The inner part of the figure illustrates cost matrix C. The red colored path indicates the optimal warping function over the cost matrix.

Human Activity Database

The recognition of head movements is based on finding the optimal alignment between two time series. A DTW based classifier was created for this reason with 26 classes of possible head movements. Let us denote a class of head movements with $M_i \subset \mathcal{M}, i \in [1:26]$, where $\mathcal{M}$ is the basic set of all possible head movements. For demonstrational purposes, the head drawn letters of the English alphabet were considered. Thus, each M_i class contains such head movements that have similar trajectories regarding the letters (e.g., the trajectories of a generates class M_0):

$$M = \{M_i \subset \mathcal{M}\}_{i \in [1:26]}, \tag{11}$$

where the classes $M_i \subset \mathcal{M}$ consist of 100 previously recorded head movements – in other words, $|M_i| = 100$. The classes are disjoint and non-empty by definition, therefore $\bigcup_{i \in [1:26]} M_i = M$.

An ordering can also be introduced for classes M_i based on the DTW distance for each movement $m_i^a, m_i^b \in M_i$ $(a, b \in [1:100], a \neq b)$. A pivot element $m_i^p \in M_i$ can be chosen based on the ordering in each class that represents its M_i class the best. Therefore, at least 26 cost matrices have to be estimated during a simple 1-NN classification of an unknown movement. Thus, every unknown movement is compared to the pivot element and the label of an unknown movement will be classified according to the pivot element that is the closest – in the sense of DTW distance – to the unknown movement. The pivot element $m_i^p \in M_i$ of the ith class can be defined as follows:

$$m_i^p = \min_D D(m_i^a, m_i^b), \tag{12}$$

where function $D(\cdot)$ is the pairwise DTW distance within the head movements of the same class M_i. Pivot element m_i^p minimizes the distance to all other elements in its class M_i, and behaves as a centroid of a cluster. Figure 9 below illustrates several moments of head movement recognition, especially the visual representation of trajectory that is only based on head pose.

Figure 9. Several moments of head movement recognition. Head movements are colored by a red-green transition, where the color of the start point is red and the current point of the trajectory is green. The shape of trajectory only depends on the head pose, more accurately the rotation around axes X and Y.

FACIAL GESTURE RECOGNITION APPLICATIONS

Facial gesture recognition has many applications. In this section, we will describe two of our existing applications where facial gesture recognition is taken into consideration. The first application is about the cross-platform development of the basis of a facial gesture recognition system. The expression cross-platform refers to the fact that the application operates in desktop and mobile environments with the same functionalities. The continuous improvement of smartphones allows us to perform computationally expensive tasks such as several computer vision algorithms. Smartphones have the ability to collect observations about users during HCI, which together with the increased computing power can have numerous benefits, for example, the access of information can be expanded and the interactions can be accomplished in a more evident way than before. Our concept is to develop a cross-platform facial gesture recognition application in order to make it run on multiple device platforms (on Windows and Android). The application logic, which contains computer vision algorithms, is shared between the different platforms and is written in C/C++. We have chosen C++ because of its advantageous properties since it gives us the opportunity to write an efficient, fast, cross-platform code, and in this way the same facial recognition algorithms have to be implemented for all platforms. An own user interface is developed for all supported platforms by using their native technologies (i.e., Java on Android). Moreover, we have also implemented a thin-layer of platform-specific C/C++ component in order to transfer data between application logic and user interfaces. This is a JNI bridge regarding the Android platform. Figure 10 below shows the architecture, but we will not give more details about it as it was described in [24]. We also described our comparative results in [24], so here we will just summarize them shortly.

We executed the same test cases on both platforms for the same application logic. The test PC is an Intel(R) Core(TM)2 Quad CPU Q9550 @ 2.83 GHz, with 4 GB RAM and the smartphone is a Samsung Galaxy S3 Neo with a Qualcomm Snapdragon 400 @ 1.4 GHz CPU and 1.5 GB RAM. We have found that the runtime is particularly influenced by the Viola and Jones face detector. The average runtime of face detection does not really differ on different platforms; it is 190 ms on PC and 240 ms on smartphone. The runtime of the other modules is not significant on PC. In contrast, the computation cost of ASM fitting is quite significant; we measured 48 milliseconds for it, which is almost ten times higher than on PC. The average runtime for a whole frame is 20 ms on PC and 84 ms on smartphone.

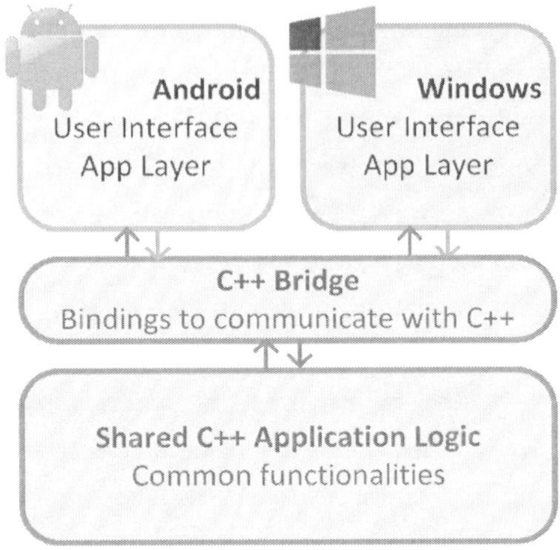

Figure 10. The architecture of our cross-platform facial gesture recognition application.

The second application is a good example for a multi-modal human-computer (HC) interface based system as in [25]. The author's goal was to build a chess playing system with multi-modal interfaces, and study whether the HC interface provides any benefits. This system was named Turk-2 after the Turkish chess-playing machine constructed in the late 18th century by Farkas Kempelen. Turk-2 is a mechanically simple robot, but by adding a face analyzer module and a talking head on a screen, it is capable of communicating in a human-like way.

This system is able to detect a human player's emotional state, recognize some simple words, and monitor the chessboard to detect moves made by the player. The output of the system is conveyed by a talking head that is capable of directing her gaze, exhibiting emotional facial expressions and performing speech with lip-sync as output. Turk-2 performs moves of the figures by a single robot arm. The authors report experimental results concluding that a system implementing HC interface appears to be more human-like and provides better game experience.

REFERENCES

[1] Lara O. D. and Labrador M. A., "A Survey on Human Activity Recognition using Wearable Sensors," *IEEE Communications Surveys & Tutorials,* vol. 15, no. 3, pp. 1192-1209, Third Quarter 2013.

[2] Viola P. and Jones M., "Rapid Object Detection using a Boosted Cascade of Simple Features," in Proceedings of the 2001 *IEEE Computer Society Conference on Computer Vision and Pattern Recognition,* vol. 1, pp. 511-518, 2001.

[3] Cootes T. F., Taylor C. J., Cooper D. H. and Graham J., "Active shape models - their training and application," *Computer Vision and Image Understanding,* vol. 61, pp. 38-59, 1995.

[4] Milborrow S. and Nicolls F., "Active Shape Models with SIFT Descriptors and MARS," in *Proceedings of the 9th International Conference on Computer Vision Theory and Applications*, pp. 380-387, 2014.

[5] Gower J. C., "Generalized procrustes analysis," *Psychometrika,* vol. 40, no. 1, pp. 33-51, 1975.

[6] Morency L. P. and Whitehill J. M. J., "Monocular Head Pose Estimation Using Generalized Adaptive View-based Appearance Model," *Image and Vision Computing*, vol. 28, no. 5, p. 754-761, 2010.

[7] Morency L. P., Whitehill J. and Movellan J., "Generalized adaptive view-based appearance model: Integrated framework for monocular head pose estimation," *8th IEEE International Conference on Automatic Face & Gesture Recognition*, pp. 1-8, 2008.

[8] Bertok K., Sajo L. and Fazekas A., "A Robust Head Pose Estimation Method Based on POSIT Algorithm," *Argumentum,* vol. 7, pp. 348-356, 2011.

[9] Bertok K. and Fazekas A., "Recognizing Complex Head Movements," *Australian Journal of Intelligent Information Processing Systems,* vol. 14, pp. 3-17, 2016.

[10] Fischler M. A. and Bolles R. C., "Random Sample Consensus: A Paradigm for Model Fitting with Applications to Image Analysis and Automated Cartography," *Communications of the ACM*, vol. 24, no. 6, pp. 381-395, 1981.

[11] Lepetit V., Noguer F. M and Fua P., "EPnP: An Accurate O(n) Solution to the PnP Problem," *International Journal of Computer Vision,* vol. 81, no. 2, pp. 155-166, 2009.

[12] Li S., Xu C. and Xie M., "A Robust O(n) Solution to the Perspective-n-Point Problem," *IEEE Transactions on Pattern Analysis and Machine Intelligence,* vol. 34, no. 7, pp. 1444-1450, 2012.

[13] C. P. Lu, G. D. Hager and E. Mjolsness, "Fast and Globally Convergent Pose Estimation from Video Images," *IEEE Transactions on Pattern Analysis and Machine Intelligence,* vol. 22, no. 6, pp. 610-622, 2000.

[14] Dementhon D. F. and Davis L. S., "Model-based Object Pose in 25 Lines of Code," *International Journal of Computer Vision*, vol. 15, no. 1, pp. 123-141, 1995.

[15] Gupta S., Markey M. K. and Bovik A. C., "Anthropometric 3D Face Recognition," *International Journal of Computer Vision*, vol. 90, no. 3, pp. 331-349, 2010.

[16] Al-Rahayfeh A. and Faezipour M., "Eye Tracking and Head Movement Detection: A State-of-Art Survey," *IEEE Journal of Translational Engineering in Health and Medicine,* pp. 11-22, 2013.

[17] Liu J. Z. and Zhao Z., "Head Movement Recognition Based on LK Algorithm and Gentleboost," *2011 7th International Conference on Networked Computing and Advanced Information Management*, pp. 232-236, 2011.

[18] Liu K., Luo Y., Tei G. and Yang S., "Attention Recognition of Drivers Based on Head Pose Estimation," *2008 IEEE Vehicle Power and Propulsion Conference,* pp. 1-5, 2008.

[19] Chutorian E. M. and Trivedi M., "Head Pose Estimation and Augmented Reality Tracking: An Integrated System and Evaluation for Monitoring Driver Awareness," *IEEE Transactions on Intelligent Transportation Systems*, vol. 11, no. 2, pp. 300-311, 2010.

[20] Bertok K. and Fazekas A., "Recognizing Human Activities Based on Head Movement Trajectories," In *Proceedings of IEEE International Conference on CogInfoCom* 2014, pp. 273-278, 2014.

[21] Bemdt D. J. and Clifford J., "Using Dynamic Time Warping to Find Patterns in Time Series," *KDD workshop*, vol. 10, no. 16, 1994.

[22] Keogh E. and Ratanamahatana C. A., "Exact Indexing of Dynamic Time Warping," *Knowledge and Information Systems*, vol. 7, no. 3, pp. 358-386, 2005.

[23] Sakoe H. C. S., "Dynamic Programming Algorithm Optimization for Spoken Word Recognition". *IEEE Transactions on Acoustics, Speech, and Signal Processing*, vol. 26, no. 1, pp. 43-49, 1978.

[24] Bertok K. and Fazekas A., "Face Recognition on Mobile Platforms," In *Proceedings of IEEE International Conference on CogInfoCom* 2016, pp. 37-43, 2016.

[25] Sajo L., Ruttkay Zs. and Fazekas A., "Turk-2, a multi-modal chess player" *International Journal of Human-Computer Studies*, vol. 69, no. 7-8, pp. 483-495, 2011.

Biographical Sketches

Kornél Bertók

Researcher

Affiliation: Faculty of Informatics, University of Debrecen, Debrecen, Hungary

Business Address: 4028 Debrecen, Kassai út 26.

Research and Professional Experience: Human-computer interactions; Object detection, recognition and categorization; Camera models, calibration and object's pose estimation; Modeling 2-D or 3-D objects; 3-D scene reconstruction;

Attila Fazekas
Associate Professor

Affiliation: Faculty of Informatics, University of Debrecen, Debrecen, Hungary

Business Address: 4028 Debrecen, Kassai út 26.

Research and Professional Experience: Human-computer interactions; Image processing, Pattern recognition, Digital topology

In: Gesture Recognition
Editors: G. Coleman and R. Ward
ISBN: 978-1-53613-491-9

Chapter 3

HAND GESTURE RECOGNITION USING FEATURE VECTORS FROM ALGEBRAIC GRAPH THEORY

***Liliane Rodrigues de Almeida**[*], **Gilson Antonio Giraldi**[†]*
***and Marcelo Bernardes Vieira**[‡]*
National Laboratory for Scientific Computing (LNCC), Brazil,
Federal University of Juiz de Fora (UFJF), Brazil

Abstract

In this work, the main goal is to explore spectral features from algebraic graph theory in static hand gesture recognition. Specifically, we apply a technique that uses the elements of the spectral matrix of the Laplacian to construct symmetric polynomials that are permutation invariants. The values of these polynomials can be used as graph features in a statistical learning pipeline that has the ability of distinguishing between distinct graphs and can reveal graph clusters. This technique avoids the correspondences between the nodes of graphs. So, we take a set of hand gestures RGB images and perform their segmentation through a graph-cuts algorithm. The obtained regions are processed for key points extraction. Next, we represent each hand region with a graph in order to compute the spectral features. In this case, we can compare the feature

[*]E-mail address: lili.rodrigues.ufjf@gmail.com.
[†]E-mail address: gilson@lncc.br.
[‡]E-mail address: marcelo.bernardes@ufjf.edu.br.

vectors, computed for different hand poses, using the Euclidean metric. The sensitivity of spectral features against graph changes will be considered in the corresponding experiments. Next, we evaluate the spectral features ability to group different gestures as different graph clusters. The results point toward the necessity of embedding the graph feature vectors in a compact space, computed by principal components analysis (PCA), followed by the linear discriminant analysis (LDA) technique to calculate the more important directions for classification. Using this approach we get suitable recognition rates for two class separating problems using K-nearest-neighbor (KNN) classifier. However, we notice a decreasing in the accuracy for multi-class problems indicating the necessity of improvements in the recognition methodology.

Keywords: pattern recognition, hand gesture, spectral features, algebraic graph theory

1. Introduction

Hand gestures are natural channels for human-to-human communication used in our everyday life. A gesture is a spatiotemporal pattern which may be classified as static or dynamic [1]. The former can be represented by a static model once the hand remains in a (almost) fixed position and configuration. On the other hand, dynamic gesture involves changes in factors such as hand orientation, velocity and fingers configuration. The area of hand gesture recognition has wide-ranging applications such as developing aids for the hearing impaired, recognizing sign language, communication in video conference, robot control, intelligent home systems, navigation and/or manipulating in virtual environments [2–5].

In this chapter, we focus on static hand gesture recognition in RGB images. In this field, hand shape localization, feature extraction and the recognition of gestures are the challenging issues [6]. Hand shape location can be achieved through segmentation techniques and template matching. Hand segmentation can be performed through skin color models [7] despite their sensitivity to variations in illumination and shadows [8]. In this area, Gaussian mixture models can also be used to capture complex variations caused by the difference of human races and gender [9]. Besides, the graph-cuts approach can be used to pose the segmentation as a binary labeling problem [10, 11]. Graph techniques are also used in the template matching proposed in [12] that, instead of relying on a separate segmentation stage, integrates hand detection with posture classification. Besides, inspired in the face detection method proposed in [13], a Viola-Jones-like hand detection scheme is combined with a color based detector, giving satisfactory results [14].

In this work we focus on segmentation based recognition pipelines. In these cases, the segmented hand should be properly represented in order to be processed correctly in further operations. This step needs the computation of geometric or image descriptors to determine the meaning of a given hand pose [15]. These features should be selected in order to take into account the variability in terms of hand position, orientation, scale, speed, and ambient lighting [16]. Besides, features can be local, if quantify characteristics of a particular region of the object, or global, if related to the whole target. In the context of static hand gesture representation, we find features computed by Zernike and pseudo Zernike moments [17], local orientation histogram, HSV models, geometric features given by the area, hand/palm and fingertips locations, and joint angles [5, 16]. Statistical features, associated with the intensity field inside the hand, like entropy, mean, skewness, standard deviation and kurtosis, have been also used [6].

In the recognition stage, the extracted features are assembled in feature vectors that serve as the input to machine learning algorithms, like support vector machine, K-nearest-neighbor (KNN), and neural networks for classification and recognition of the hand gestures [18]. For real world applications it is important that the recognition works despite complex cluttered backgrounds. This fact motivates the application of deep learning methods for hand detection and hand gesture recognition [19, 20]

In this chapter, we aim to explore the combination of a graph-cuts technique for segmentation, spectral features from algebraic graph theory, and machine learning algorithm in static hand gesture recognition. So, we take a set of RGB hand gestures images and perform their segmentation through a graph-cuts methodology [21]. The obtained regions are processed for boundary and skeleton extraction in order to select a set of key points in the segmented hand. Instead of skeleton, we can apply the scale invariant feature transform (SIFT) algorithm to select inner key points [22]. The key points will be used in the following stage to build a Delaunay graph whose nodes are the extracted points. Then, we compute spectral features, from algebraic graph theory, to represent each hand pose.

Specifically, we apply the technique described in [23] that uses the elements of the spectral matrix for the Laplacian to construct symmetric polynomials that are permutation invariants. As a consequence, this technique avoids the correspondences between the nodes of graphs when comparing different poses. Also, as observed in [23], these polynomials, when evaluated over the spectral matrix columns, can be used as graph features in a statistical learning approach that has the ability of distinguishing between distinct graphs. In this scenario, the sensitivity of spectral features against graph changes must be considered in order to simulate small hand changes as well as artifacts generated due to segmentation problems. Then, we apply the KNN technique to evaluate the spectral features ability to distinguish different gestures as different graph classes. However, we noticed that the KNN cannot efficiently distinguish sample groups using the high dimensional and complex feature space generated. Hence, dimensionality reduction and discriminant analysis should be performed for discarding redundancies and selection of important features to pattern recognition tasks [24,25].

In this avenue, we follow a statistical learning approach whose basic pipeline includes [26]: (a) Linear subspace learning for dimensionality reduction; (b) Compute discriminant directions for separating sample groups in classification tasks. So, we embed the graph feature vectors in a compact space, computed by principal components analysis (PCA), and followed by the linear discriminant analysis (LDA) technique to select the more important directions for classification. Using this approach we get suitable classification rates for two-class separating problems using KNN together with k-fold cross validation method. However, we notice a decreasing in the accuracy for multi-class problems indicating the necessity of improvements in the recognition methodology for static hand gesture classification.

The chapter is organized as follows. Section 2 discusses the main ideas behind the segmentation methodology. In Section 3, we review basic elements in graph theory. Next, Section 4 presents basic theory about symmetric polynomials. Section 5 describes the proposed methodology. Computational experiments are presented on Section 6. Section 6.3 gives the conclusions and future directions for this work.

2. Hand Segmentation By Graph-Cuts

We are interested in finding signs performed directly by hand, without any covering such as gloves. In this specific case, segmentation methods focusing in skin detection are useful. Many methods and models have been proposed in literature to represent and segment human skin. Based on [21], we propose to use graph-cuts to robustly segment skin in color images.

Given a RGB image $I : \mathcal{V} \longrightarrow \mathbb{R}^3$, were $\mathcal{V} \subset \mathbb{R}^2$ is a set of pixels arranged in a regular grid, we need to find the characteristic function $X : \mathcal{V} \longrightarrow \{0, 1\}$ which is the minimum argument of a function [27] that encodes the skin information. A common objective function for image segmentation is the Gibbs energy ([28, 29]) defined as:

$$E(X) = \sum_{v_i \in \mathcal{V}} E_1(X(v_i)) + \lambda \sum_{(v_i, v_j) \in \mathcal{E}} E_2(X(v_i), X(v_j)), \tag{1}$$

where v_i e v_j represent pixels (or elements) to be segmented, $\mathcal{E}$ is the set of connected elements depending on the image topology and λ is a weight. E_1 is the term that defines a cost for each v_i to belong to one of the sets. This cost should be inversely proportional to the probability of v_i to belong to the set. It is usually:

$$\begin{array}{lll} E_1(X(v_i) = 1) = 0, & E_1(X(v_i) = 0) = \infty, & \forall v_i \in O, \\ E_1(X(v_i) = 1) = \infty, & E_1(X(v_i) = 0) = 0, & \forall v_i \in B, \\ E_1(X(v_i) = 1) = \phi(\rho_o), & E_1(X(v_i) = 0) = \phi(\rho_f), & \forall v_i \in \mathcal{N}, \end{array} \tag{2}$$

where O is a set of object pixels, B is the background elements, $\mathcal{N}$ is the set of pixels with unknown label and ϕ is a function inversely proportional to its arguments ρ_o and ρ_f. E_2 is a term that defines a penalty for two connected elements (v_i, v_j) with opposite labels. This penalty depends on the similarity of both pixels. A bigger similarity means that the pixels have high probability of belonging to the same set.

2.1. Hand Skin Database

As proposed in [21], we use n_s images of hand poses for training the graph-cuts where skin regions and non-skin regions are explicitly marked by an user. The idea is to use these multiple images to infer the likelihood of a pixel color to represent a skin. In our approach, the color space used was *Lab* instead of RGB since it gave better segmentation results with hand pose databases [30].

In each image I_i, $0 < i \leq n_s$, of the training database, n_o pixels are marked as skin, forming an object region $O_i \subsetneq I_i$, and n_b pixels are marked as background, forming a region $B_i \subsetneq I_i$. Note that $O_i \cup B_i$ is not necessarily a partition of I_i, i.e., not all pixels must be labeled.

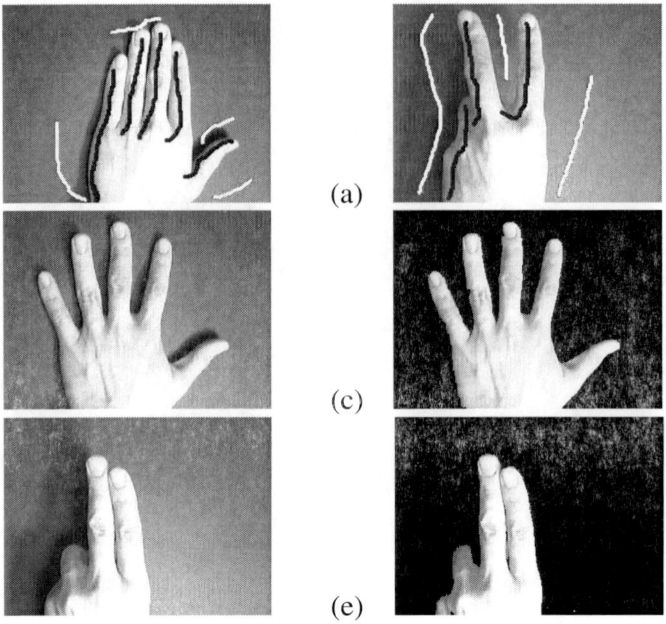

Figure 1. Example of skin based hand pose segmentation. (a)-(b) Training set examples with object (black) and background (white) pixels marked. (c)-(f) Segmentation results on images not included in training data set.

The database is then represented by n_s sets, each one composed by k_o colors of O_i and k_b colors of B_i. These k_o and k_b colors are computed using a quantization method capable of finding the best colors to represent each sub region gamut. We use the k-means method for simplicity. The n_s images work as a supervised training set for finding the probability distributions needed to minimize equation (1).

2.2. Skin Segmentation

Let $CO_{m,i}$ be the m-th mean object color and $CB_{l,i}$ be the l-th mean background color of the i-th training image, where $0 < m \leq k_o$, $0 < l \leq k_b$ and $0 < i \leq n_s$. It is possible to define the similarities with the following equations:

$$\begin{aligned} d_{o,i} &= min_m||C_v - CO_{m,i}||, \\ d_{b,i} &= min_l||C_v - CB_{l,i}||, \end{aligned}$$

where C_v is the color of the pixel v that we need to label as skin or not, $d_{o,i}$ and $d_{b,i}$ are the minimum distance between C_v and the colors of the i-th object set and the colors of the $i-th$ background set in the training database, respectively.

Similar to [28], our energy terms for the equation (1) are then defined as:

$$E_1(X(v)=1)=\frac{1}{n_s}\sum_{i=1}^{n_s}\frac{d_{o,i}}{d_{o,i}+d_{b,i}}, \tag{3}$$

$$E_1(X(v)=0)=\frac{1}{n_s}\sum_{i=1}^{n_s}\frac{d_{b,i}}{d_{o,i}+d_{b,i}}, \tag{4}$$

$$E_2(X(v_1),X(v_2))=\frac{|X(v_1)-X(v_2)|}{||C_{v_1}-C_{v_2}||^2+1}, \tag{5}$$

where C_{v_1} and C_{v_2} are the colors of neighbor pixels v_1 and v_2. The term $|X(v_1) - X(v_2)|$ makes $E_2(X(v_1), X(v_2)) = 0$ whenever v_1 and v_2 belong to the same set. The energy E_1 penalizes a pixel belonging to a skin or non-skin sets, whereas E_2 gives the penalty when v_1 and v_2 pixels are assigned with different labels.

In the test stage, this method is applied directly in new color images to find skin regions. No skin or background labels are needed for the test images. The energy terms were conceived to gather skin and non-skin information only from the database images.

In this approach, the marked images can be viewed as a training set to define the energy terms (equations (3)-(5)). Indeed, it is important to mark as many types of skins as possible under different illumination conditions. Equally important is to pick as many distinct background regions as possible. Of course, the variation of background colors is expected to be much higher than the skin colors in outdoor scenes with natural backgrounds. However, our experiments show that even controlled indoor environments can have high color variations for both foreground and background. So, the training set is thus crucial for this method to give good skin segmentation. Despite its simplicity, however, a well defined data set and clustering parameters can provide fairly good skin segmentation even with complex background scenes.

3. Spectral Graph Theory

Consider the undirected graph $\mathcal{G} = (\mathcal{V}, \mathcal{E})$ with node set $\mathcal{V} = \{v_1, v_2, \ldots, v_n\}$, having no loops, with set of edges $\mathcal{E} = \{e_{ab} = (v_a, v_b)\} \subset \mathcal{V} \times \mathcal{V}$. The adjacency matrix $\mathbf{A}$ for the graph $\mathcal{G}$ is the $n \times n$ matrix with elements:

$$A_{ij} = \begin{cases} 1 & if \ (v_a, v_b) \in \mathcal{E}, \\ 0 & otherwise. \end{cases} \tag{6}$$

Hence, the Laplacian of the graph is given by $\mathbf{L} = \mathbf{D} - \mathbf{A}$, where $\mathbf{D}$ is the diagonal node degree matrix whose element $D_{ii} = \sum_{j=1}^{n} A_{ij}$ gives the number of edges which exit the individual node v_i. The Laplacian is more suitable for spectral analysis than the adjacency matrix since it is positive semidefinite besides symmetric. Therefore, it has eigenvalues which are all either positive or zero. Let $\mathbf{e}_i$, $i = 1, 2, \ldots n$ be the eigenvectors of $\mathbf{L}$ with corresponding eigenvalues λ_i, $i = 1, 2, \ldots n$. Hence, we can perform the eigenvector expansion for the Laplacian matrix:

$$\mathbf{L} = \sum_{i=1}^{n} \lambda_i \mathbf{e}_i \mathbf{e}_i^T, \tag{7}$$

which allows to define the spectral matrix as the one with the scaled eigenvectors as columns:

$$\Phi = \begin{pmatrix} \sqrt{\lambda_1}\mathbf{e}_1 & \sqrt{\lambda_2}\mathbf{e}_2 & \ldots & \sqrt{\lambda_n}\mathbf{e}_n \end{pmatrix}. \tag{8}$$

Due to expression (7) we can show that:

$$\mathbf{L} = \Phi\Phi^T. \tag{9}$$

Two graphs $\mathcal{G}^1 = \left(\mathcal{V}^1, \mathcal{E}^1\right)$ and $\mathcal{G}^2 = \left(\mathcal{V}^2, \mathcal{E}^2\right)$ which contain the same number of nodes (say, $\mathcal{V}^1 = \left\{v_1^1, v_2^1, \ldots, v_n^1\right\}$ and $\mathcal{V}^2 = \left\{v_1^2, v_2^2, \ldots, v_n^2\right\}$) are isomorphic if there is a permutation $\pi : \mathcal{V}^1 \rightarrow \mathcal{V}^2$ (bijective function $\pi : \mathcal{V}^1 \rightarrow \mathcal{V}^2$) such that $\left(v_i^1, v_j^1\right) \in \mathcal{E}^1$ if and only if $\left(\pi\left(v_i^1\right), \pi\left(v_j^1\right)\right) \in \mathcal{E}^2$; that means, $\mathcal{G}^1$ and $\mathcal{G}^2$ have the same topology. In this case, if $\mathbf{L}$ and $\overline{\mathbf{L}}$ are the Laplacian matrices of $\mathcal{G}^1$ and $\mathcal{G}^2$, respectively, then we can build $\overline{\mathbf{L}}$ through a permutation of both rows and columns of $\mathbf{L}$ generating the matrix $\overline{\mathbf{L}} = \mathbf{P}\mathbf{L}\mathbf{P}^T$, where $\mathbf{P}$ is a permutation matrix, obtained from the identity matrix $\mathbf{I}$ by permuting the rows or columns.

Clearly, there is a family of Laplacian matrices which can be transformed into one another using permutation matrices. The spectral matrix is also modified by permutations, but this operation only reorders the rows of the matrix $\mathbf{L}$. In fact, let $\overline{\Phi} = \mathbf{P}\Phi$. Then:

$$\overline{\Phi\Phi}^T = \mathbf{P}\Phi\Phi^T\mathbf{P}^T = \mathbf{PLP}^T = \overline{\mathbf{L}}. \tag{10}$$

An important property of the eigenvalues of $\mathbf{L}$ is that they are not changed by the application of a permutation matrix. To demonstrate this, we shall notice that, if $\mathbf{Le} = \lambda\mathbf{e}$ and $\bar{\mathbf{e}} = \mathbf{Pe}$, we have:

$$\overline{\mathbf{L}}\bar{\mathbf{e}} = \mathbf{PLP}^T\mathbf{Pe} = \mathbf{PLe} = \lambda\mathbf{Pe} = \lambda\bar{\mathbf{e}}, \tag{11}$$

which means that, λ is also an eigenvalue of the Laplacian matrix $\overline{\mathbf{L}}$. Consequently, the Laplacian matrix eigenvalues have been used as a compact spectral representation for comparing graphs [31]. Moreover, the eigenvalues can be computed from the spectral matrix using the identity [32]:

$$\lambda_j = \sum_{i=1}^{n} \Phi_{ij}^2, \quad j = 1, 2, \ldots n. \tag{12}$$

4. Symmetric Polynomials

Let $\mathbb{P}_n$ be the group of permutations $\pi : \{1, 2, \ldots, n\} \rightarrow \{1, 2, \ldots, n\}$, also called the symmetric group on n things. Besides, consider the set of polynomials in the independent variables $\{v_1, v_2, \ldots, v_n\}$ denoted by $\mathbb{Z}[v_1, v_2, \ldots, v_n]$. Let $\pi \in \mathbb{P}_n$ act on $\mathbb{Z}[v_1, v_2, \ldots, v_n]$ by:

$$\pi(v_i) = v_{\pi(i)}. \tag{13}$$

In the above context, we say that a polynomial $f(v_1, v_2, \ldots, v_n) \in \mathbb{Z}[v_1, v_2, \ldots, v_n]$ is symmetric, or invariant under $\mathbb{P}_n$, if for all $\pi \in \mathbb{P}_n$:

$$f(\pi(v_1), \pi(v_2), \ldots, \pi(v_n)) = f(v_1, v_2, \ldots, v_n). \tag{14}$$

There is a special set of these polynomials, referred to as the elementary symmetric polynomials $S_r = S_r(\upsilon_1, \upsilon_2, \ldots, \upsilon_n)$, $r = 1, 2, \ldots, n$, which is defined as:

$$S_1(\upsilon_1, \upsilon_2, \ldots, \upsilon_n) = \sum_{i=1}^{n} \upsilon_i, \tag{15}$$

$$S_2(\upsilon_1, \upsilon_2, \ldots, \upsilon_n) = \sum_{i=1}^{n} \sum_{j=i+1}^{n} \upsilon_i \upsilon_j, \tag{16}$$

$$S_r(\upsilon_1, \upsilon_2, \ldots, \upsilon_n) = \sum_{i_1 < i_2 < \ldots < i_r}^{n} \upsilon_{i_1} \upsilon_{i_2} \ldots \upsilon_{i_r}, \tag{17}$$

$$S_n(\upsilon_1, \upsilon_2, \ldots, \upsilon_n) = \prod_{i=1}^{n} \upsilon_i. \tag{18}$$

A fundamental result in this theory is summarized in the theorem below that gives a way to express symmetric polynomial in terms of the elementary ones.

Theorem 1. A polynomial $f \in \mathbb{Z}[\upsilon_1, \upsilon_2, \ldots, \upsilon_n]$ is invariant under $\mathbb{P}_n$ if and only if it can be written as:

$$f(\upsilon_1, \upsilon_2, \ldots, \upsilon_n) = g(S_1(\upsilon_1, \upsilon_2, \ldots, \upsilon_n), S_2(\upsilon_1, \upsilon_2, \ldots, \upsilon_n), \ldots, S_n(\upsilon_1, \upsilon_2, \ldots, \upsilon_n)), \tag{19}$$

where $g \in \mathbb{Z}[\upsilon_1, \upsilon_2, \ldots, \upsilon_n]$.

Sketch of the Proof. Induction in n.

(a) For $n = 1$ it is trivial.

(b) Induction:

- Hypothesis: It is true for $n - 1$.
- Thesis: It is true for n. Let a symmetric polynomial $f \in \mathbb{Z}[\upsilon_1, \upsilon_2, \ldots, \upsilon_n]$. Then, the function $h(\upsilon_1, \upsilon_2, \ldots, \upsilon_{n-1}) = f(\upsilon_1, \upsilon_2, \ldots, \upsilon_{n-1}, 0)$ is a symmetric

polynomial. By the induction hypothesis, there is a polynomial $g \in \mathbb{Z}[v_1, v_2, \ldots, v_{n-1}]$ such that $h(v_1, v_2, \ldots, v_{n-1}) = g(S_1(v_1, v_2, \ldots, v_{n-1}), S_2(v_1, v_2, \ldots, v_{n-1}), \ldots, S_{n-1}(v_1, v_2, \ldots, v_{n-1}))$. Let:

$$\tilde{h}(v_1, v_2, \ldots, v_{n-1}, v_n) =$$
$$g(S_1(v_1, v_2, \ldots, v_{n-1}, v_n), \ldots, S_{n-1}(v_1, v_2, \ldots, v_{n-1}, v_n)).$$

From construction, it is clear that:

$$f(v_1, v_2, \ldots, v_{n-1}, 0) - \tilde{h}(v_1, v_2, \ldots, v_{n-1}, 0) = 0.$$

As a consequence, v_n divides $\left[f(v_1, v_2, \ldots, v_{n-1}, v_n) - \tilde{h}(v_1, v_2, \ldots, v_{n-1}, v_n)\right]$ which, in turn, is a symmetric polynomial. Therefore, every v_i divides this expression and, consequently:

$$\frac{f - \tilde{h}}{S_n} = \frac{f(v_1, v_2, \ldots, v_{n-1}, v_n) - \tilde{h}(v_1, v_2, \ldots, v_{n-1}, v_n)}{S_n(v_1, v_2, \ldots, v_{n-1}, v_n)}, \tag{20}$$

is a polynomial in $\mathbb{Z}[v_1, v_2, \ldots, v_n]$ with lower total degree than the original f. Another induction in the total degree of expression (20) completes the proof (see [33] for details). ■

The power symmetric polynomial functions:

$$P_r(v_1, v_2, \ldots, v_n) = \sum_{i=1}^{n} v_i^r, \quad r = 1, 2, \ldots n, \tag{21}$$

are related to the elementary symmetric polynomials and offer an efficient algorithm to compute them, through the Newton-Girard formula, that gives the relationship between these two polynomial sets [34]:

$$S_r = \frac{(-1)^{r+1}}{r} \sum_{k=1}^{r} (-1)^{k+r} P_k S_{r-k}, \; r = 1, 2, \ldots, n, \tag{22}$$

where $P_k = P_k(v_1, v_2, \ldots, v_n)$, $k = 1, 2, \ldots, n$.

To demonstrate expression (22) we shall remember that:

$$\ln(1 - zv_i) = -\sum_{j=1}^{\infty} \frac{(zv_i)^j}{j}.$$

Therefore:

$$\exp \sum_{i=1}^{n} \ln(1 - zv_i) = \exp\left(-\sum_{j=1}^{\infty} z^j \frac{\sum_{i=1}^{n} (v_i)^j}{j}\right) = \exp\left(-\sum_{j=1}^{\infty} z^j \frac{P_j}{j}\right).$$

So, by applying the exponential property $(\exp(a+b) = \exp(a)\exp(b))$ and expanding 'exp' in Taylor series we obtain:

$$\exp \sum_{i=1}^{n} \ln(1 - zv_i) = \prod_{j=1}^{\infty} \exp\left(-z^j \frac{P_j}{j}\right) = \prod_{j=1}^{\infty} \left(\sum_{k=0}^{\infty} \frac{1}{k!} \left(-z^j \frac{P_j}{j}\right)^k\right). \tag{23}$$

However, we can demonstrate that [35]:

$$\exp \sum_{i=1}^{n} \ln(1 - zv_i) =$$

$$\sum_{j=0}^{\infty} z^j \sum_{l_1+2l_2+\ldots+nl_n=j} \frac{(-P_1/1)^{l_1}}{l_1!} \frac{(-P_2/2)^{l_2}}{l_2!} \frac{(-P_3/3)^{l_3}}{l_3!} \cdots \frac{(-P_n/n)^{l_n}}{l_n!}. \tag{24}$$

On the other hand:

$$\exp \sum_{i=1}^{n} \ln(1 - zv_i) = \prod_{i=1}^{n} (1 - zv_i) = \sum_{j=1}^{n} (-1)^j S_j z^j. \tag{25}$$

From equations (24)-(25), if we set $S_0 = 1$, we get that:

$$\sum_{j=0}^{n} (-1)^j S_j z^j =$$

$$\sum_{j=0}^{\infty} z^j \sum_{l_1+2l_2+\ldots+nl_n=j} \frac{(-P_1/1)^{l_1}}{l_1!} \frac{(-P_2/2)^{l_2}}{l_2!} \frac{(-P_3/3)^{l_3}}{l_3!} \cdots \frac{(-P_n/n)^{l_n}}{l_n!}. \tag{26}$$

Therefore, we obtain the following expressions for $j \leq 3$:

(a) Case $j = 0$: Trivial.

(b) Case $j = 1$:

$$1 - S_1 z = 1 - \frac{P_1}{1!} \Rightarrow S_1 = P_1 = \frac{(-1)^{1+1}}{1} \sum_{k=1}^{1} (-1)^{1+1} P_1 S_{1-1}. \quad (27)$$

(c) Case $j = 2$:

$$S_2 = \sum_{l_1+2l_2=2} \frac{(-P_1/1)^{l_1}}{l_1!} \frac{(-P_2/2)^{l_2}}{l_2!} = \frac{(P_1)^2}{2!} - \frac{P_2}{2}. \quad (28)$$

However, by using the result (27) and replacing $S_1$to P_1 into (28) we obtain:

$$S_2 = \frac{1}{2}(P_1)^2 - \frac{P_2}{2} = \frac{(-1)^{2+1}}{2} \sum_{k=1}^{2} (-1)^{k+2} P_k S_{2-k}. \quad (29)$$

(d) Case $j = 3$:

$$-S_3 = \sum_{l_1+2l_2+3l_3=3} \frac{(-P_1/1)^{l_1}}{l_1!} \frac{(-P_2/2)^{l_2}}{l_2!} \frac{(-P_3/3)^{l_3}}{l_3!}. \quad (30)$$

Consequently, from this expression and the equations (27)-(29), it is straightforward to show that:

$$S_3 = +\frac{(P_1)^3}{3!} - \frac{P_1}{1!}\frac{P_2}{2} + \frac{P_3}{3} = \frac{(-1)^{3+1}}{3} \sum_{k=1}^{3} (-1)^{k+3} P_k S_{3-k}. \blacksquare$$

Therefore, we have checked the relationship (22) for $0 \leq j \leq 3$. The complete demonstration can be found in [34].

A remarkable fact is that it is possible to recover the values of υ_i given the values of the elementary symmetric polynomials [23]. This is demonstrated by observing that the polynomial equation:

$$\prod_{i=1}^{n} (x - \upsilon_i) = 0, \quad (31)$$

has solutions $\upsilon_1, \upsilon_2, \ldots, \upsilon_n$. By expanding (31) we get:

$$x^n - S_1 x^{n-1} + S_2 x^{n-2} + \ldots + (-1)^n S_n = 0. \tag{32}$$

So, by substituting the values of expressions (15)-(18) into (32), and finding the roots, we can recover, up to a permutation, the original values of υ_i.

5. Proposed Methodology

Using the theory of Section 4 and the approach presented in [23], the graph features S_r are constructed as follows: we substitute $\upsilon_1 = \Phi_{1i}$, $\upsilon_2 = \Phi_{2i}$, ..., $\upsilon_n = \Phi_{ni}$ into expressions (15)-(18) and produce the polynomials $S_1(\Phi_{1i}, \Phi_{2i}, \ldots, \Phi_{ni})$, $S_2(\Phi_{1i}, \Phi_{2i}, \ldots, \Phi_{ni})$,..., $S_n(\Phi_{1i}, \Phi_{2i}, \ldots, \Phi_{ni})$. The values of these polynomials are invariant under permutations of the node labels. Also, once $i = 1, 2, \ldots, n$ we can construct a set of n^2 spectral features using the n columns of the spectral matrix Φ in combination with the n symmetric polynomials. Moreover, from the definition of the spectral matrix we know that $\Phi = \{\Phi_{ij}\} = \{\sqrt{\lambda_j} e_{ij}\}$, $1 \leq i, j \leq n$. Therefore, considering expressions (15)-(18) we obtain:

$$S_{1j} = \sum_{i=1}^{n} \Phi_{ij} = \sum_{i=1}^{n} \sqrt{\lambda_j} e_{ij} = \sqrt{\lambda_j} \left(\sum_{i=1}^{n} e_{ij} \right), \tag{33}$$

$$S_{2j} = \sum_{i<k}^{n} \Phi_{ij} \Phi_{kj} = \sum_{i<k}^{n} \sqrt{\lambda_j} e_{ij} \sqrt{\lambda_j} e_{kj} = \sum_{i<k}^{n} \sqrt{\lambda_j \lambda_j} \left(e_{ij} e_{kj} \right), \tag{34}$$

$$\vdots$$

$$S_{rj} = \sum_{i_1<i_2<\ldots<i_r}^{n} \Phi_{i_1 j} \Phi_{i_2 j} \ldots \Phi_{i_r j} = \sum_{i_1<i_2<\ldots<i_r}^{n} \sqrt{(\lambda_j)^r} \left(e_{i_1 j} e_{i_2 j} \ldots e_{i_r j} \right), \tag{35}$$

$$\vdots$$

$$S_{nj} = \prod_{i=1}^{n} \Phi_{ij} = \prod_{i=1}^{n} \sqrt{\lambda_j} e_{ij} = \sqrt{(\lambda_j)^n} \left(e_{1j} e_{2j} \ldots e_{nj} \right). \tag{36}$$

According to [23], the distribution of S_{rj}, for large r, is highly non-Gaussian with a dominant tail. It happens due to the product terms involving $\sqrt{(\lambda_j)}^r$ that appear in the higher order polynomials in expressions (33)-(36). In order to balance the distribution, we follow [23] and perform the transformation:

$$F_{ij} = signum\left(S_j\left(\Phi_{1i}, \Phi_{2i}, \ldots, \Phi_{ni}\right)\right) \ln\left(1 + \left|S_j\left(\Phi_{1i}, \Phi_{2i}, \ldots, \Phi_{ni}\right)\right|\right),$$

where $1 \leq i, j \leq n$. The feature vector is build by assembling the rows of the matrix $\{F_{ij}\}$ to generate the vector:

$$\mathbf{B} = \left(F_{11}, F_{12}, \ldots, F_{1n}, F_{21}, F_{22}, \ldots, F_{2n}, \ldots, F_{n1}, F_{n2}, \ldots, F_{nn}\right). \quad (37)$$

The computation of the feature vector in equation (37) depends on the elementary symmetric polynomials, given by expressions (15)-(18). To efficiently perform this task, given a set of variables $\{v_1, v_2, \ldots, v_n\}$, we apply the Newton-Girard formula (22).

The proposed pipeline for static hand gesture recognition is composed by the following steps: (a) Convert RGB images in the Lab color system; (b) Hand segmentation based on graph-cuts technique of Section 2; (c) The result is used as a mask to bound the region of interest in the RGB image; (d) Convert the region of interest in grayscale; (e) Extract key points; (e) Graph construction using the key points as nodes; (f) Feature vector generation through expression (37); (g) Apply PCA for dimensionality reduction; (h) LDA discriminant directions computation. (e) Classification using KNN in the LDA feature space.

The first step was motivated by the observation that the hand patterns are better represented in the Lab color system as we can notice when comparing Figures 2(a) and 2 (b). The graph-cuts technique for hand segmentation needs a training stage, in which we take sample images from the database and specify the object of interest as well as the background through a few marking lines (see Figure 1 (a)-(b)) by dragging the mouse cursor while holding a button (left button indicating the foreground, and right button for the background). The colors in the marked points are used to parameterize the graph-cuts energies used in equation (1). Then, given a new image of the database in the Lab system (Figure 2 (b)), the segmentation is automatically performed. The obtained binary image (Figure 2 (c)) is used as a mask to select the region of interest in the corresponding grayscale image, as pictured in Figure 2 (d).

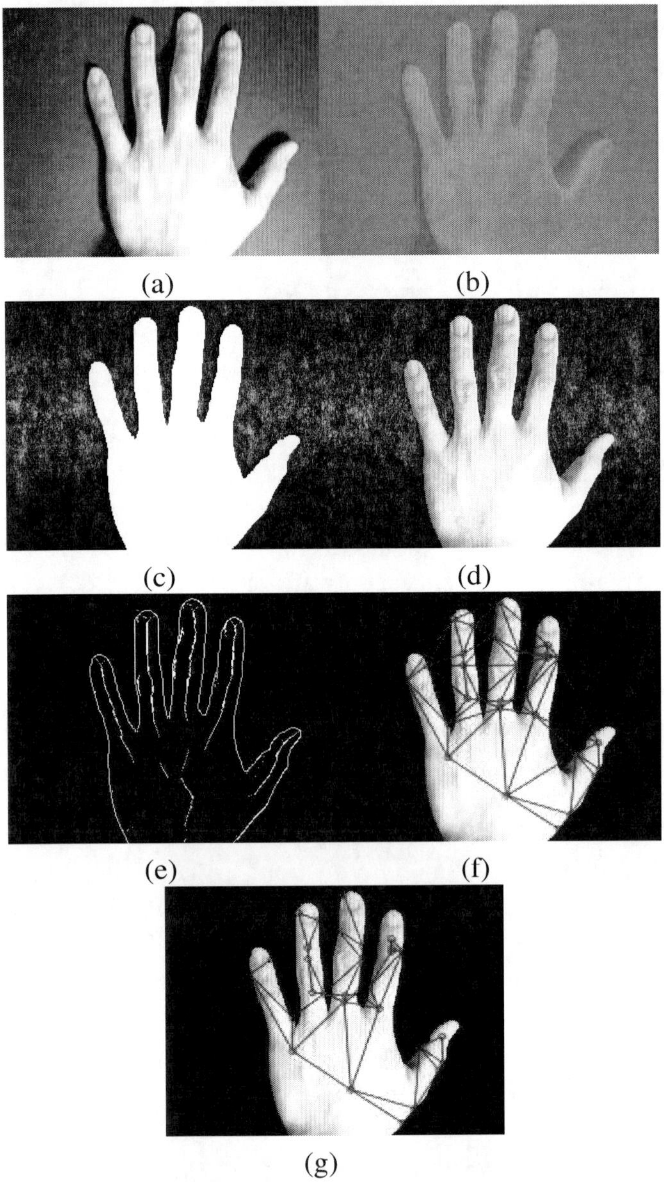

Figure 2. Pipeline for Delaunay triangulation: (a) Database image in grayscale; (b) Grayscale visualization of the hand image in the *Lab* system; (c) Segmented image (mask); (d) Region of interest in grayscale; (e) Skeleton and object boundary; (f) Delaunay triangulation using key points; (g) Constrained Delaunay triangulation.

The next stage computes key points using a subset of the skeleton as well as boundary points in the binary image. The skeleton of a region in a binary image can be obtained through morphological operations. So, given a $2D$ structuring element B and a binary set X we can define the simplest morphological transformations, named erosion and dilation, as follows:

$$X \ominus B = \{x; \quad B_x \subset X\}, \tag{38}$$

$$X \oplus B = \{x; \quad B_x \cap X \neq \emptyset\}, \tag{39}$$

where B_x denotes the translation of B so that its origin is located at the pixel x, $X \ominus B$ means the erosion of X by B and $X \oplus B$ means the dilation of X by B. In this framework, the skeleton of a $2D$ object X can be obtained by [36]:

$$S(r) = \cup_r (X \ominus rB) - [(X \ominus rB) \odot B], \tag{40}$$

where $rB = B \oplus \cdots \oplus B$ r times and '$\odot$' means the opening of X by the structuring element B, defined by:

$$X \odot B = (X \ominus B) \oplus B. \tag{41}$$

The Figure 2 (e) pictures the skeleton and boundary points extracted from the mask in Figure 2 (c). Instead of the skeleton, we could also use the SIFT methodology to get inner key points [22]. Among the main steps of SIFT algorithm we find: (i) Local extreme detection in scale-space; (ii) Key points localizations. In (i) it uses the convolution of an image $I(x, y)$ with a Difference-of-Gaussian function with standard-deviation σ in order to identify candidate points to be invariant to scale changes:

$$DoG(x, y, \sigma) = (G(x, y, k\sigma) - G(x, y, \sigma)) * I(x, y) = L(x, y, k\sigma) - L(x, y, \sigma). \tag{42}$$

In equation (42), the symbol '$*$' denotes the traditional convolution operation, k is an integer parameter, $G(x, y, \sigma)$ is the $2D$ Gaussian function with standard-deviation σ:

$$G(x, y, \sigma) = \frac{1}{2\pi\sigma^2} \exp\left(-\frac{x^2 + y^2}{2\sigma^2}\right). \tag{43}$$

and $L(x, y, \sigma)$ stands for the smoothed image $G(x, y, \sigma) * I(x, y)$. The last stage of step (i) is a methodology for the detection of local maxima and minima of

$DoG(x, y, \sigma)$. In (ii) the low contrast points are rejected and undesirable edge responses are eliminated. This process allows a robust key point extraction process less sensitive to illumination and scale variations.

The subset of points extracted through the skeleton or SIFT is combined with boundary points and the result is processed by triangulation algorithm, which generates a Delaunay graph having those points as nodes, as visualized in Figure 2(f). Finally, the constrained Delaunay graph is yielded (Figure 2(g)) by removing the graph edges that cross the background.

The spectral feature vectors, computed through expression (37), are processed by PCA technique for dimensionality reduction. The PCA is one of the most successful approaches to the problem of creating a low dimensional data representation and interpretation. Since the pioneering work of Sirovich and Kirby [37], several subsequent works have projected data on a PCA space for dimensionality reduction of the original samples for further classification and analysis. Given the feature vectors $\mathbf{B}_i \in \mathbb{R}^{n^2}$, $i = 1, 2, \ldots, N$, the PCA algorithm is composed by the following steps:

1. Global mean: $\overline{\mathbf{B}} = \frac{1}{N}\sum_{i=1}^{N} \mathbf{B}_i$.

2. $\widetilde{\mathbf{B}}_i = \mathbf{B}_i - \overline{\mathbf{B}}$.

3. $\mathbf{C} = \sum_{i=1}^{N} \widetilde{\mathbf{B}}_i . \widetilde{\mathbf{B}}_i^T$.

4. Compute the eigenvectors $\{\mathbf{e}_1, \mathbf{e}_2, \cdots, \mathbf{e}_{n^2}\}$ of $\mathbf{C}$ and select the d ones with the largest eigenvalues to compose the projection matrix, say $\mathbf{P_{pca}} = \left[\begin{array}{cccc} \mathbf{e}_1 & \mathbf{e}_2 & \ldots & \mathbf{e}_d \end{array}\right] \in \mathbb{R}^{n^2 \times d}$.

5. Calculate the projected vectors: $\widehat{\boldsymbol{B}}_i = \mathbf{P_{pca}}^T \widetilde{\mathbf{B}}_i$.

However, since PCA explains the covariance structure of all the data its most expressive components, that is, the first principal components with the largest eigenvalues, are not necessarily the most discriminant ones [38]. A common practice to identify the important linear directions for separating sample groups in general is to use Fisher's Linear Discriminant Analysis (LDA) [39,40]. When the dimension of the feature space is greater than the number of groups, LDA can find number of groups - 1 meaningful discriminant directions [41].

Let the scatter matrices between-class $\mathbf{C}_b$ and within-class $\mathbf{C}_w$ be defined, respectively, as

$$\mathbf{C}_b = \sum_{i=1}^{g} n_i(\widehat{\boldsymbol{B}}_i)(\widehat{\boldsymbol{B}}_i)^T \tag{44}$$

and

$$\mathbf{C}_w = \sum_{i=1}^{g}\sum_{j=1}^{n_i}(\widehat{\mathbf{B}}_{i,j} - \widehat{\overline{\mathbf{B}}}_i)(\widehat{\mathbf{B}}_{i,j} - \widehat{\overline{\mathbf{B}}}_i)^T, \tag{45}$$

where $\widehat{\mathbf{B}}_{i,j}$ is the d-dimensional PCA pattern j from class i, n_i is the number of training patterns from class i, and g is the total number of classes or groups. The vector $\widehat{\overline{\mathbf{B}}}_i$ is the unbiased mean of class i [40].

The main objective of LDA is to find a projection matrix $\mathbf{W}_{lda}$ that maximizes the ratio of the determinant of the between-class scatter matrix to the determinant of the within-class scatter matrix (Fisher's criterion), that is:

$$\mathbf{W}_{lda} = \arg\max_{W} \frac{|\mathbf{W}^T C_b \mathbf{W}|}{|\mathbf{W}^T \mathbf{C}_w \mathbf{W}|}. \tag{46}$$

The Fisher's criterion described in equation (46) is maximized when the projection matrix $\mathbf{W}_{lda}$ is composed of the eigenvectors of $\mathbf{C}_w^{-1}\mathbf{C}_b$ with at most $(g-1)$ nonzero corresponding eigenvalues [39, 40]. Finally, the classification is performed by projecting each $\widehat{\boldsymbol{B}}_i$ using the matrix $\mathbf{W}_{lda}$:

$$\boldsymbol{Y}_i = \mathbf{W}_{lda}^T \widehat{\boldsymbol{B}}_i, \tag{47}$$

where $\boldsymbol{Y}_i \in \mathbb{R}^{g-1}$ in the full rank case.

6. Computational Experiments

In these experiments, we have used the Cambridge hand-gesture data set [42], which has 900 RGB image sequences of 2 subjects, with nine different hand gesture classes, encompassing 100 image sequences per class. Each sequence was recorded in front of a fixed camera having roughly isolated gestures in space and time. The gesture data are collected based on rotation and hand contraction movements. Besides, illumination changes are considered generating five different sets, each one acquired under a different illuminations condition. The Figure 3 shows (in grayscale) the 9 classes of gestures, based on 3 movements (rotations leftward/rightward and hand contraction) and 3 primitive hand shapes, under the same illumination setup.

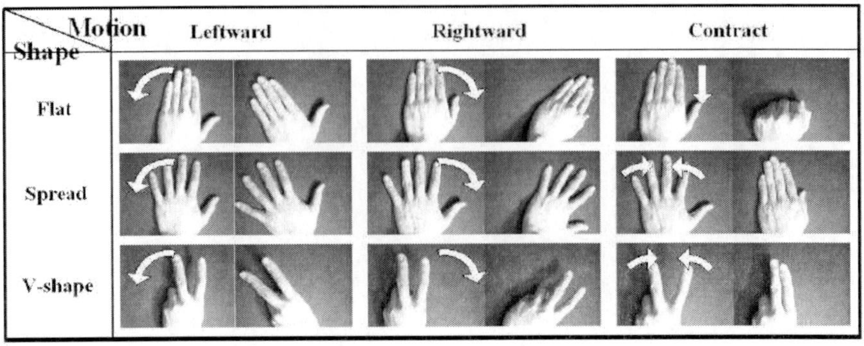

Figure 3. Cambridge data set: nine gesture classes generated by three different shapes and movements (source [43]).

In this section, we intend to evaluate the spectral features ability to group different static gestures as different graph clusters and the recognition rates obtained by the methodology presented in Section 5. To build a suitable data set, we assume that the flat shape in Figure 3 and its leftward/rightward motions are variations of the same static gesture. Following an analogous point of view for the others basic shapes (spread and V-shape) in Figure 3, we build three static gesture classes. Besides, we take two contract hand poses of the last column of Figure 3. In this way, we extract from the hand configurations of the Cambridge database a total of five classes represented in Figure 4. We select 30 images from each class to perform the segmentation and recognition experiments.

The hand segmentation is performed using the graph-cuts methodology explained in Section 2, available in the OpenCV 3.3.0. In the training step of graph-cuts, the major task is to encode color similarities that indicate if a pixel belongs to the foreground or background. Hence, we select a subset of $n_s = 5$ hand images and allow the user to use lines and curves to specify the foreground object against its background. Each curve on the image is drawn by dragging the mouse cursor while holding the left button to indicate the foreground or the right button for the background. The pixels over these lines are displayed in white or black colors for the background or foreground markers, respectively.

However, following the methodology explained in Section 5, before this process we convert the original images to the Lab color system. The Figures 5 (a)-(c) pictures three samples of the Cambridge database, their representation in the Lab system (Figure 5 (d)-(f)) and the curves traced by the user, shown in

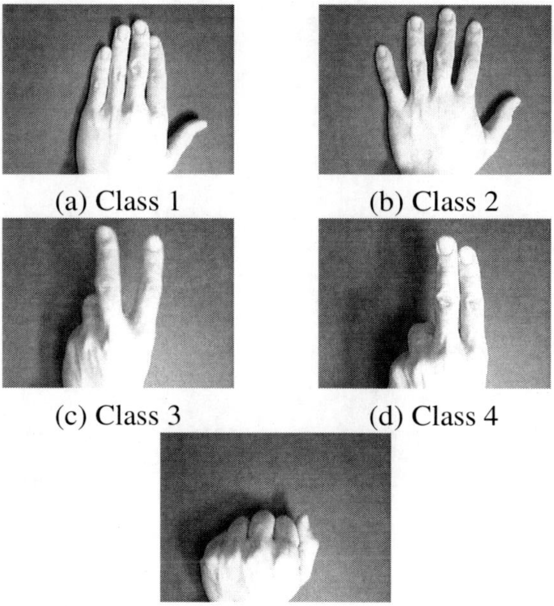

(a) Class 1 (b) Class 2

(c) Class 3 (d) Class 4

(e) Class 5

Figure 4. Gesture classes, up to rotations and contractions, used in our experiments, and labeled as $1, 2, 3, 4, 5$, as indicated.

Figures 5 (g)-(i).

Once the user marks the training images in the Lab color system, we compute the mean object/background colors $CO_{m,i}$ and $CB_{l,i}$, respectively, where $0 < m \leq k_o$, $0 < l \leq k_b$ and $0 < i \leq 5$ (see Section 2.2). For the Cambridge database, we experimentally set $k_o = 16$, $k_b = 8$. So, given a test image I of the database, the mean color sets are used to compute the energy E_1, defined by expressions (3)-(4), in the Lab color system. The energy due to the image gradient along the object boundary is computed by equation (5). The segmentation process is represented in Figures 2 (a)-(d), which show in grayscale the original image (Figure 2 (a)), the corresponding Lab color field in Figure 2 (b), and the final segmentation represented by the binary image in Figure 2 (c). This image allows to extract the region of interest in the original image, converted to grayscale image, as pictured in Figure 2 (d).

Then, we take the image in Figure 2 (d) and select a sequence of key points using the boundary/skeleton of the region of interest. SIFT can be also used

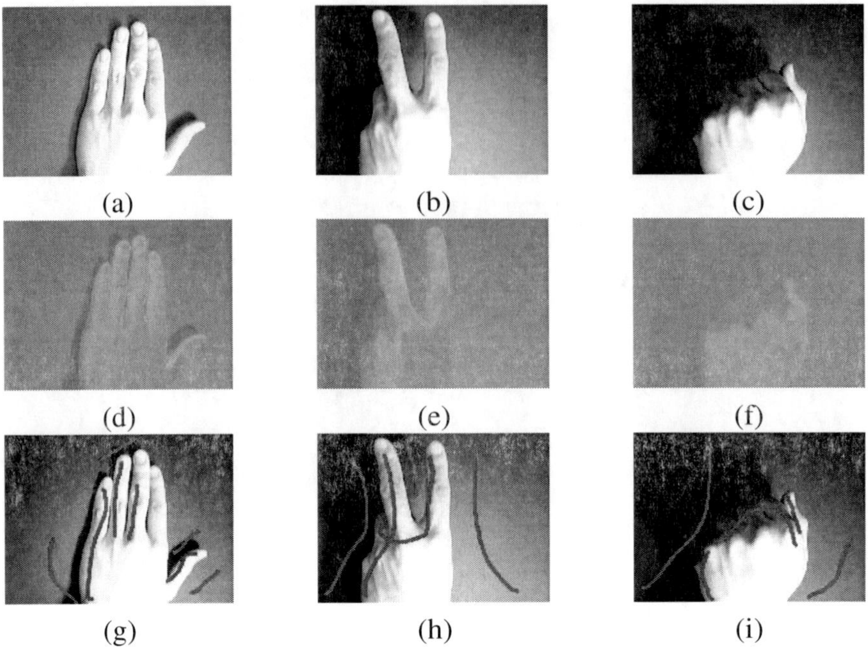

Figure 5. Training process of graph-cuts: (a)-(c) Database images in grayscale. (d)-(f) Conversion to Lab system with visualization in grayscale. (g)-(i) Curves drawn by the user to distinguish the background (white lines) from the foreground (black lines).

instead of skeleton. The key points are input to build the Delaunay graph, shown in Figure 2 (f). The final triangulation of the hand region, shown in Figure 2 (g), is obtained by removing the graph edges that cross the background (black region). Each so obtained triangulation is represented by a feature vector $\mathbf{B}$, computed through expression (37).

In the whole training (Figure 5) and test processes, we identify issues related to the graph-cuts parameterization and spectral features sensitivity to segmentation problems which affect the representation capabilities of the feature vector B in expression (37). Besides, we shall analyze the performance of the classification approach proposed in Section 5.

6.1. Graph-Cuts Parameterization and Illumination Changes

Firstly, let us consider some definitions attached to the characteristic function X and a graph representation of a digital image.

Definition 1. Let $\mathcal{G} = (\mathcal{V}, \mathcal{E})$ be the grid-graph representing a digital image, defined by the triangulation of Figure 6. The line graph of $\mathcal{G}$, denoted by $\mathcal{G}^l$, is the graph whose vertex set is the edge set $\mathcal{E}$ and, given two vertices, they are adjacent if and only if they have one common vertex in $\mathcal{V}$.

Definition 2. We call an edge $e_{ab} = (v_a, v_b)$ of the graph $\mathcal{G} = (\mathcal{V}, \mathcal{E})$ *completely labeled* respected to X if this function changes its value in e_{ab}.

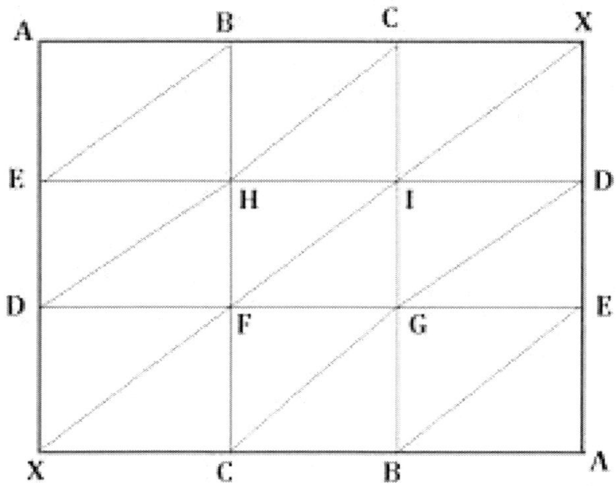

Figure 6. Image representation using a triangulation whose nodes are image pixels.

We know from the discrete and polyhedral geometry that in the grid-graph representation given by the triangulation of the Figure 6, the set of completely labeled edges can be decomposed into a set of closed paths in $\mathcal{G}^l$ [44]. Consequently, the graph-cuts solution partitions the entire image into a set of disjoint and connected regions [45]. The properties of such segmentation are controlled by the degrees of freedom in the graph-cuts which depend on the numbers k_o and k_b of color clusters in the foreground and background, respectively, as well as the parameter λ, all of them used in expression (1). So, in this section we analyze the performance of the graph-cuts segmentation when applied to samples of the five gesture classes in Figure 4, the sensitivity of the solution against variations of k_o, k_b, λ, and robustness of the segmentation against variations in illumination.

The setting of parameters is through trial and error. The Figure 7 shows the hand segmentation for the five images picture on Figure 4 with $k_o = 16$, $k_b = 8$, and $\lambda = 1000$. A visual inspection shows that the precision of the results is very good.

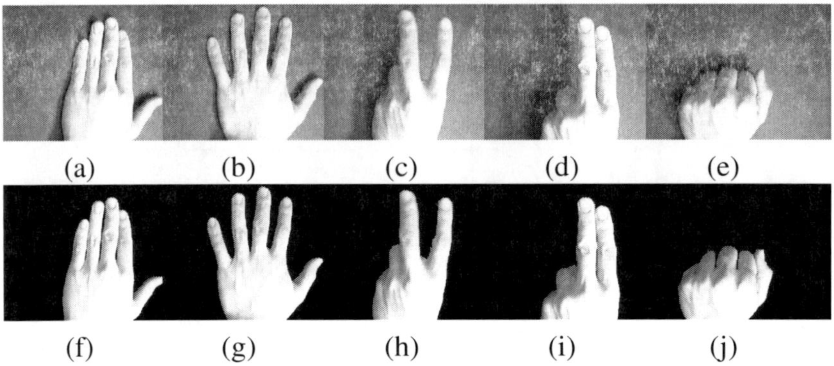

Figure 7. Graph-cuts solutions: (a)-(e) Original images in grayscale. (f)-(j) Segmentation results.

Now, we repeatedly modify the graph-cuts parameters and evaluate the result. Hence, we consider each segmentation in Figure 7 as a ground truth, compute the graph-cuts result with new parameters, and compare the two segmentations by measuring the similarity between them. Formally, let the ground truth segmentation S_g be represented by the partition $\left(S_g^f, S_g^b\right)$, where S_g^f and S_g^b denote the object of interest (foreground) and background, respectively. Analogously, let S_t be the segmentation being evaluated, that is represented by the partition $\left(S_t^f, S_t^b\right)$. In this scenario, we can compare S_g and S_t through the Jaccard index:

$$JAC\left(S_g, S_t\right) = \frac{|S_g^f \cap S_t^f|}{|S_g^f \cup S_t^f|}, \tag{48}$$

where $|.|$ means the number of pixels of the argument region. Due to the expression (48), we shall notice that $0 \leq JAC\left(S_g, S_t\right) \leq 1$, and it ideally is one when the segmentations match correctly while zero indicates no similarity.

In the following examples we start from the ground truth segmentations of Figures 7 (a)-(e), obtained with $k_o = 16$, $k_b = 8$, and $\lambda = 1000$, and change the parameters as indicated on Table 1. In order to avoid a combinatorial explosion in the number of possibilities to test, we decided to take the ground truth parameters and to set two values for λ, say λ_1 and λ_2, such that $\lambda_1 < 1000 < \lambda_2$. Also, we decrease the value of k_o used to get the ground truth segmentations to compose one graph-cuts setup together with k_b and λ_1. Also, we increase k_b and keep k_o unchanged respect to the ground truth, when using λ_2 in the segmentation model. The parameter values are shown in Table 1, as well as the corresponding JAC index.

Table 1. JAC index (equation (48)) for different parameters setting in the graph-cuts model with segmentations in Figure 7 as the ground truth

	Fig. 7 (a)	Fig. 7 (b)	Fig. 7 (c)	Fig. 7 (d)	Fig. 7 (e)
λ_1	100	100	100	100	100
(k_o, k_b)	$(8, 8)$	$(8, 8)$	$(8, 8)$	$(8, 8)$	$(8, 8)$
JAC	0.983	0.980	0.977	0.985	0.987
λ_2	5000	5000	5000	5000	5000
(k_o, k_b)	$(16, 20)$	$(16, 20)$	$(16, 20)$	$(16, 20)$	$(16, 20)$
JAC	0.987	0.978	0.985	0.987	0.989

The results reported in Table 1 shows low sensitivity of graph-cuts solution with the parameters changing, which is a desired feature for the model. Figure 8 allows a comparison between the graph-cuts result of Figure 7 (h) , obtained with $k_o = 16$, $k_b = 8$, $\lambda = 1000$, and the segmentation result of the same image (reproduced in Figure 8 (a)) when considering the parameters of Table 1. A visual inspection confirms the stability of the graph-cuts solution against parameter variation, numerically quantified through the high values of JAC index in Table 1. So, we perform the remaining experiments with $k_o = 16$, $k_b = 8$, $\lambda = 1000$ that give suitable results as shown in Figure 7.

The next examples allow to analyze the influence of illumination changes in the hand segmentation obtained by graph-cuts. Hence, we take the hand poses in the Figure 4, under different illumination setups, and perform their segmentation. The Figures 9 (a)-(e) picture the input images while Figures 9

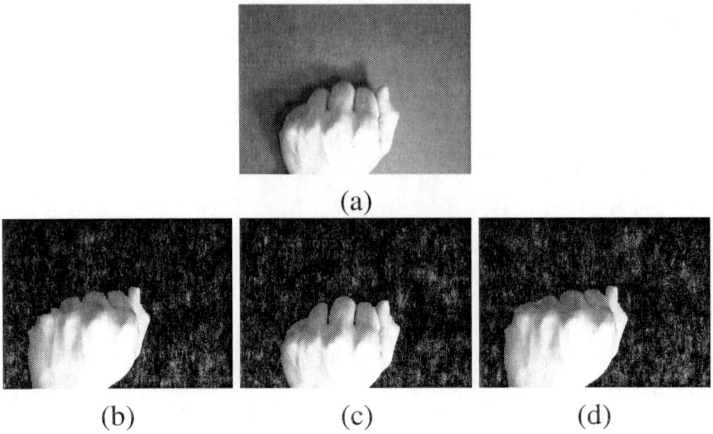

Figure 8. (a) Original image. (b) Graph-cuts result with $k_o = 8$, $k_b = 8$, and $\lambda = 100$. (c) Result using $k_o = 16$, $k_b = 8$, and $\lambda = 1000$. (d) Segmentation with $k_o = 16$, $k_b = 20$, and $\lambda = 5000$.

(f)-(j) show the segmentation results. We apply the segmentation technique with parameters $k_o = 16$, $k_b = 8$, and $\lambda = 1000$, as already mentioned before.

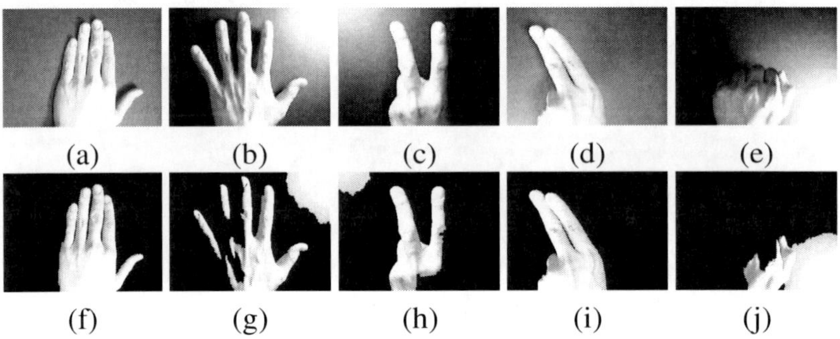

Figure 9. Graph-cuts solutions under different illumination conditions: (a)-(e) Input images in grayscale. (f)-(j) Segmentation results using graph-cuts.

These situations may cause graph-cuts to fail due to the changing in the color distribution of the image field. In fact, we can notice in Figures 9 (g),(h),(j) the detection of many false positive (background pixels detected as foreground ones) as well as false negative (foreground pixels detected as background ones). However, the segmentation in Figures 9 (f),(i) are pretty good. Consequently, under smooth conditions of illumination, like in Figure 9 (a),(d), the obtained results indicate robustness of the graph-cuts solutions.

6.2. Spectral Features Analysis

Following the methodology of Section 5, the hand regions obtained by the graph-cuts are processed for key points extraction for further graph representation and spectral features computation steps. So, this section discusses issues related to the graph generation and sensitivity of spectral features against hand/graph changes considering variation intra/inter classes.

Hence, in the first test, we take the classes 1 and 3, represented by the Figures 4 (a) and 4 (c), and perform the following experiment: (i) Select 30 image from each class; (ii) Segmentation using graph-cuts; (iii) Boundary extraction; (iv) Skeleton computation; (v) Selection of n key points randomly distributed along the boundary and skeleton; (vi) Delaunay graph generation; (vii) Delete edges that cross the background; (viii) Spectral features computation through expression (37).

In the step (v) we set $n \in \{20, 30, \cdots, 70\}$. The step (viii) generates a set of 30 feature vectors for each class, namely $\mathbf{B}_{i,j}$, $i = 1, 2, \cdots, 30, j \in \{1, 3\}$. Then, we randomly remove a percentage $p\%$, with $p \in \{5, 10, 20, 25, 50, 75\}$ of edges, generating new features vectors $\mathcal{B}_{i,j}^{p,n}$, and compute the Euclidean distances:

$$d_{i,j}(p, n) = ||\mathbf{B}_{i,j} - \mathcal{B}_{i,j}^{p,n}||. \tag{49}$$

in order to study the effect of this operation in the intra-class feature vectors distribution. The statistics of the obtained results are summarized in the boxplots shown in Figure 10.

In order to analyze the results of the Figure 10, we compute the following relative interval:

$$R = \frac{median_{max} - median_{min}}{d_{max} - d_{min}}, \tag{50}$$

where $median_{max}$ and $median_{min}$ are the maximum and minimum median values while d_{max}, d_{min} denote the maxium/minimum distance reported in each boxplot. Table 2 reports the obtained ranges. According to this table, the sensitivity against edge removal is more noticeable for the graphs with number of nodes in the set $\{20, 30, 40\}$ for both classes. The case $n = 50$ is the least sensitive, followed by the cases $n \in \{60, 70\}$. In order to study the feature vectors

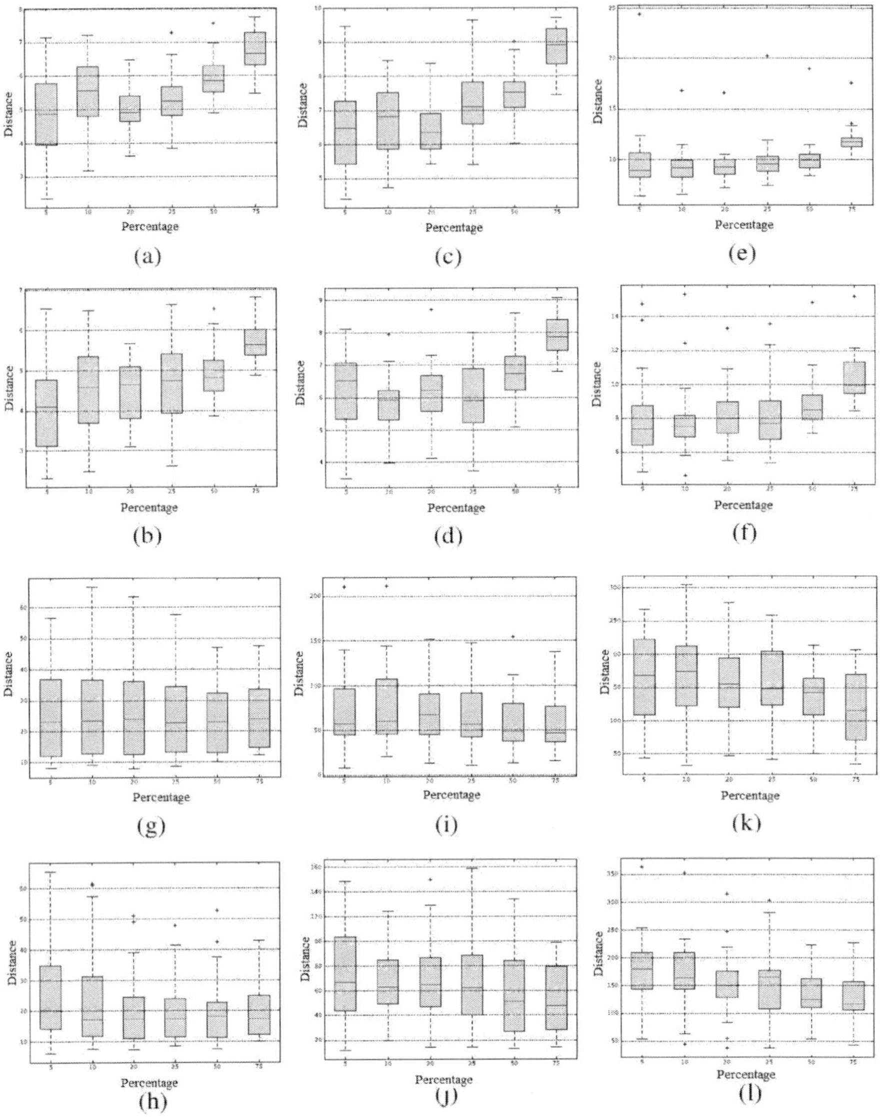

Figure 10. Distribution of the distances $d_{i,j}(p,n)$, computed by expression (49) for $p \in \{5, 10, 20, 25, 50, 75\}$ and: (a) Class $j = 1$, number of key points $n = 20$. (b) Class $j = 3$, number of key points $n = 20$. (c) $j = 1$, $n = 30$. (d) $j = 3$, $n = 30$. (e) $j = 1$, $n = 40$. (f) $j = 3$, $n = 40$. (g) $j = 1$, $n = 50$. (h) $j = 3$, $n = 50$. (i) $j = 1$, $n = 60$. (j) $j = 3$, $n = 60$. (k) $j = 1$, $n = 70$. (l) $j = 3$, $n = 70$.

Table 2. Relative interval R, computed by equation 50 with $median_{min}$, $median_{max}$, d_{min}, d_{max} given by m-min, m-max, d-min, d-max, respectively

Fig. 10	(a)	(b)	(c)	(d)	(e)	(f)	(g)	(h)	(i)	(j)	(k)	(l)
R	0.33	0.36	0.44	0.33	0.46	0.32	0.002	0.05	0.07	0.13	0.03	0.26
m-min	4.9	4.1	6.5	5.9	8.75	7.5	24.0	17.0	60.0	48	115	115
m-max	6.7	5.7	8.9	7.8	12	10	23.9	20.05	70	68	125	180
d-min	2.4	2.4	4.3	3.3	6.0	4.75	6.0	5.0	10	10.0	25.0	30.0
d-max	7.8	6.8	9.7	9.1	13	12.5	67.0	67.0	150.0	160	316	280

space under more complex setups, we decided to use $n = 30$ in the remaining experiments.

Now, we would like to analyze the capabilities of **B** space for recognizing sample of the classes in Figure 4. In this way, we perform one experiments using the KNN classification technique and k-fold cross validation method with $k = 6$. Hence, the data is divided into six subsets, and the main loop is repeated six times. Each iteration takes one of the six subsets as the test set and the other five subsets to form a training set. Then, the average accuracy across all $k = 6$ trials is computed. The results, reported in Figure 11 (a) for $K = 1$ in the classifier, indicates that the spectral features are not efficient to put similar structures close together and dissimilar ones far apart for hand gesture recognition. Besides, we notice in Figure 11 (a) that the classification performance gets worse when increasing the number g of classes from $g = 2$ to $g = 5$.

Considering the plot in Figure 11 (a), we decided to use PCA in order to obtain a more compact representation for the spectral features vectors and, consequently, discard possible redundancies. Once the number of nodes is set to $n = 30$, we generate a feature space with dimension $n^2 = 900$. Due to the fact that we have 150 samples (30 for each class), the full rank PCA subspace has at most 149 principal components. Figure 11 (b) shows the samples projected on the first two principal components. In this subspace, PCA clearly fails to recover the important features for separating the sample groups. The first principal components that maximize the total scatter across all the samples encode variations that are not enough to distinguish the classes in this case. This fact points towards the necessity of a discriminant analysis technique to compute important directions to separate different classes. That is why we have included the LDA in the proposed pipeline of Section 5, that is considered in the next section.

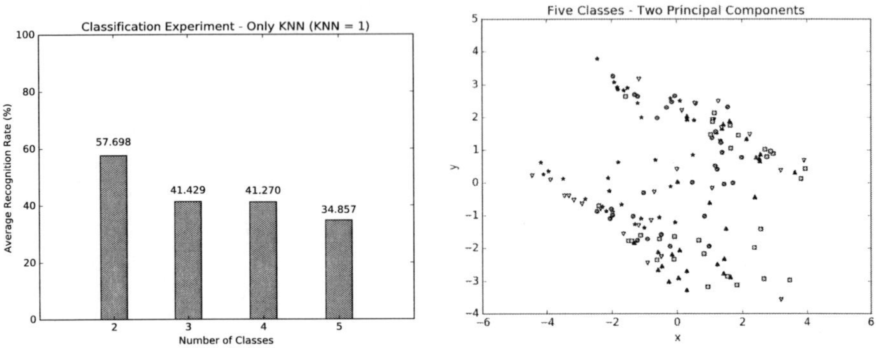

(a) (b)

Figure 11. (a) KNN accuracy, with $K = 1$, using 6-fold cross validation. (b) Projection of the samples of class 1 (black triangle), class 2 (star), 3 (black ball), 4 (square), and class 5 (upside-down triangle) in the two-dimensional most expressive subspace identified by PCA.

6.3. Discriminant Space for Spectral Features

In this section, we have investigated the effectiveness of the statistical learning pipeline that uses the feature vectors $\mathbf{B}$ (expression 37) as input, computes the PCA (steps 1-5 of Section 5), and apply LDA in the PCA space in order to get at most $g-1$ discriminant directions to project the data (expression 47). In the last stage, we use the KNN classifier, with $K \in \{1, 3, 5\}$ and Euclidian distance, to analyze the performance of the discriminant feature spaces for recognition using the classes represented in Figure 4. The obtained results are shown in Figure 12, where in the horizontal axis we indicate the number of principal components taken (denote by n_{pca} in this section) and in the vertical axis we report the average recognition rates (accuracy). The experiments with number of classes $g = 2$ use classes pictured in Figures 4 (a) and 4 (c). For $g = 3$, the classes used correspond to Figures 4 (a),(c),(e). When $g = 4$ we take all the classes shown in Figure 4 with exception of Figure 4 (d).

The Figure 12 (a) shows the average recognition rates of the 6-fold cross validation experiments, for $g = 2$, obtained by setting $K = 1$ in the KNN algorithm, using the PCA+LDA features space. We must notice from the lines in Figure 12 (a) that the features computed by the LDA technique allow higher recognition rates than the ones observed in Figure 11 (a). For instance, the plots

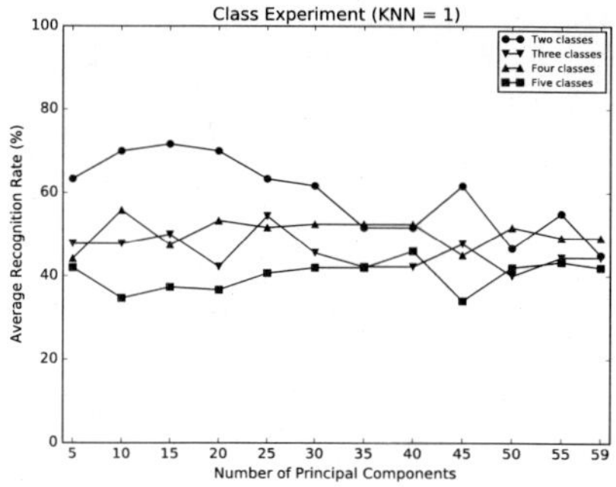

(a)

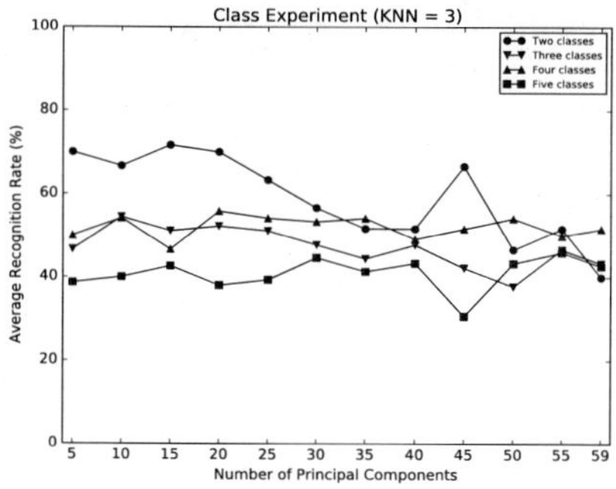

(b)

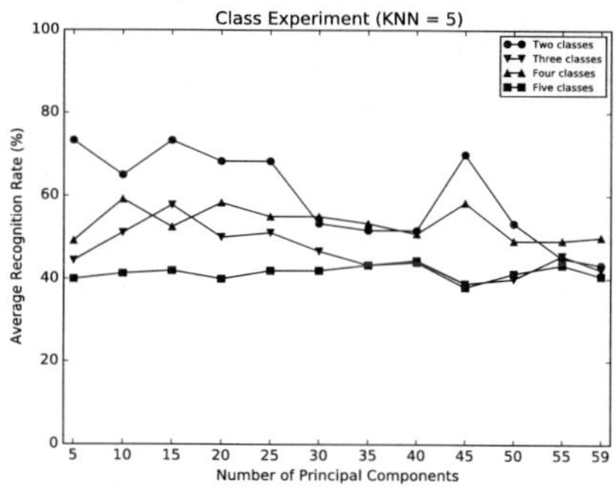

(c)

Figure 12. Recognition rates of KNN with PCA+LDA features and 6-fold cross validation. (a) Classification using $K = 1$. (b) Results with $K = 3$. (c) Accuracy using $K = 5$.

in Figure 12 (a) show that with the first 5 most expressive PCA components, the recognition rates achieved in the LDA space are better or equal than the corresponding recognition rates of spectral feature space reported in Figure 11 (a). Also, $n_{pca} = 5$ gives the highest average recognition rate observed in the experiments reported in Figure 12, given by 73.3% for $K = 5$ $g = 2$ (line with disks in Figure 12 (c)). To simplify the analysis, we have assembled in Table 3 (a) the maximum/minimum recognition rates using the combination PCA+LDA. Moreover, in Table 3 (b) we report the values of n_{pca} where the recognition pipeline achieves the maximum and minimum accuracies.

When comparing the recognition rates against the increase in the number g of classes, we notice from the plots in Figure 12 (a) a performance degradation when going from $g = 2$ to $g = 3$ and from $g = 4$ to $g = 5$, which is quantified through Table 3 (a). However, the comparison between plots with triangles of Figure 12 (a) does not show such behavior. In fact, Table 3 (a) shows that the minimum/maximum recognition rates get higher when increasing the number of classes from $g = 3$ to $g = 4$ for $K = 1$. Moreover, Figure 12 (b)-(c) show analogous characteristics for experiments with $K \in \{3, 5\}$ which is also verified in the corresponding lines of Table 3 (a).

Respect to the accuracy against the number n_{pca} of PCA components, we can notice a performance degradation for two-classes experiment (line with disks in Figure 12) if $n_{pca} > 15$, for $K \in \{1, 3\}$, and if $n_{pca} > 5$, for $K = 5$, with some oscillation for $n_{pca} > 40$, with a local maximum when $n_{pca} = 45$ in all cases.

A similar behavior is observed for $g = 3$ regarding the decreasing in the accuracy for larger PCA subspaces (lines with upside-down triangles in Figure 12) which is also highlighted in Table 3, considering that the minimum accuracy reported happens for $n_{pca} \geq 45$. However, the oscillations for $K > 40$ are less noticeably than for the two-classes case. Besides, we shall point out that the performance of the methodology for $g = 5$ falls in the range $[30.7, 46.0]$, as we can read in Table 3 (a), which is far from the acceptable, indicating the necessity of improvements (see Section 6.3). The lines with squares in Figure 12 show the evolution of the average recognition rates against the n_{pca} for 5-classes tests. The minimum accuracy happens for $n_{pca} = 45$ for all K values. If we remove this point from the lines with squares, we notice a smooth variation of the accuracy when changing the subspace dimensions of PCA. Besides, in this case, the maximum recognition rates happen for larger number of PCA components ($n_{pca} \geq 40$), as reported in Table 3 (b).

Moreover, from Table 3 (a) we notice that, the best recognitions rates for $g \in \{2, 3, 4\}$ was achieved for $K = 5$ with lower subspace dimensions ($n_{pca} \leq 15$). For $g = 5$ both $K = 1$ and $K = 3$ achieves the maximum recognition rate in the magenta plots (46.0%) although the former needs less PCA components ($n_{pca} = 40$ against $n_{pca} = 55$ for the latter) to get this result.

The Figure 13 allows to analyze the performance behavior of our recognition methodology, against the number of PCA components, if we fix the number of classes but vary the K value. Let R_1, R_3, and R_5 be the recognition rates obtained by KNN for $K = 1$, $K = 3$, and $K = 5$, respectively. If we sort these values, we notice from Figure 13 (a) that R_3 is the median for almost all the PCA subspaces for two-classes experiments. Besides, the highest recognition

Table 3. (a) Minimum and maximum accuracies for each g-classes test shown in Figure 12 (b) The n_{pca} corresponding to the minimum/maximum accuracies

g	2	3	4	5
$K = 1$	$[45.0, 71.7]$	$[40.0, 54.4]$	$[44.2, 55.8]$	$[34.0, 46.0]$
$K = 3$	$[40.0, 71.7]$	$[37.8, 54.4]$	$[46.7, 55.8]$	$[30.7, 46.0]$
$K = 5$	$[43.3, 73.3]$	$[38.9, 57.8]$	$[49.2, 59.2]$	$[38.0, 44.0]$

(a)

g	2	3	4	5
$K = 1$	59 15	50 25	5 10	45 40
$K = 3$	59 15	50 10	15 20	45 55
$K = 5$	59 5	45 15	5 10	45 40

(b)

rates are obtained by $K = 5$ in the Figures 13 (a)-(b), as also reported in Table 3 (a). The accuracy R_3 in Figure 13 (b) is the median of the three recognition rates for $n_{pca} \in \{5, 15, 25, 45, 59\}$ and R_3 outperforms the other recognition rates for $n_{pca} \in \{10, 20, 30, 35, 40, 55\}$. Also, R_1 is higher than R_3 and R_5 if $n_{pca} \in \{5, 25, 45, 59\}$.

Considering Figure 13 (c), we notice that R_5 gives better recognition rates for $n_{pca} \in \{10, 15, 20, 25, 30, 45\}$, besides been the (global) maximum accuracy in this case ($g = 4$), according to Table 3 (a). Moreover, R_1 outperforms R_2 and R_3 only for $n_{pca} = 40$, while R_3 achieves higher recognition rates than R_1 and R_5 for $n_{pca} \in \{5, 35, 50, 55, 59\}$.

The results reported in Figure 13 (d), which considers $g = 5$, show that R_5 outperforms the other recognition rates for $n_{pca} \in \{10, 20, 25, 35, 45\}$. In the other eight subspaces, the rates R_1 and R_3 get better results achieving the (global) maximum in the 5-classes experiment for $n_{pca} = 40$ and $n_{pca} = 55$, respectively (see also Tables 3 (a)-(b)).

In the last test we analyze the performance of the proposed methodology (Section 5) when replacing the skeleton to SIFT to form, together with the boundary points, the set of key points. To perform this task, we consider the best and worst setups reported in Table 3 (a), given, respectively, by ($g = 2, K = 5$) and ($g = 5, K = 5$). We keep the number of key points $n = 30$, which are

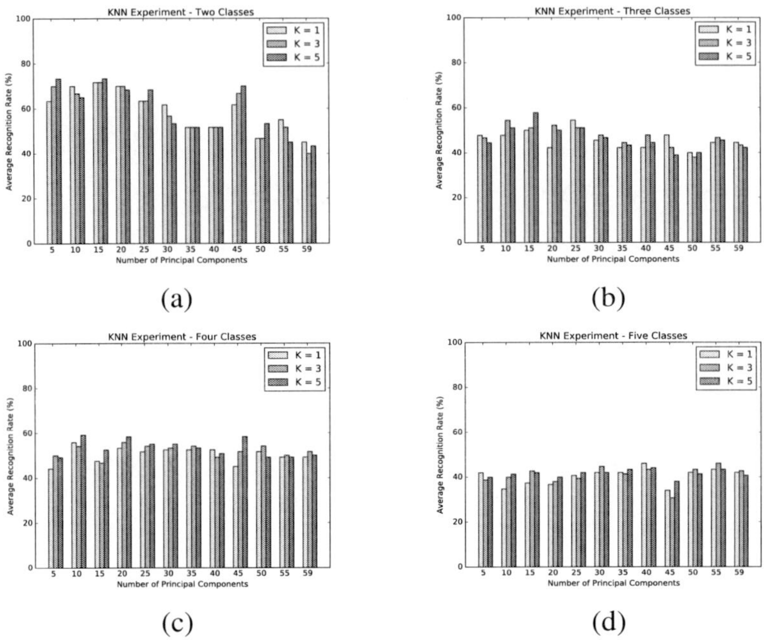

Figure 13. (a) Binary classification using classes 1 and 3 (see Figures 4 (a) and 4 (c)) in the LDA features space. (b) Three-class experiment with classes in Figures 4 (a),(c),(e). (c) Four-class average recognition rates using classes in Figures 4 (a),(b),(c),(e). (d) Result for classes 1-5 of Figure 4.

randomly distributed along the boundary and the SIFT points. We execute the SIFT algorithm (Section 5) over the graph-cuts results and select only SIFT key points in the interior of the region of interest. The average recognition rates are shown in Figure 14. Despite of some similarities between Figures 14 (a)-(b) and the blue and magenta plots in Figure 12 (c), the Tables 4 and 3 (a) report that the maximum recognition rate for 2-classes experiment decreases when using SIFT (from 73.3% to 71.7%) but it gets higher for 5-classes test (from 44.0% to 46.7%). In this case, we notice that the PCA subspace dimensions where the maximum rates are achieved are $n_{pca} = 40$ when using the skeleton and $n_{pca} = 50$ if taking inner points through SIFT. Therefore, we get some improvement in the recognition for 5-classes experiments (from 44.0% to 46.7%) with the price of increasing the computational cost for recognition, due to the increase in the PCA subspace dimension.

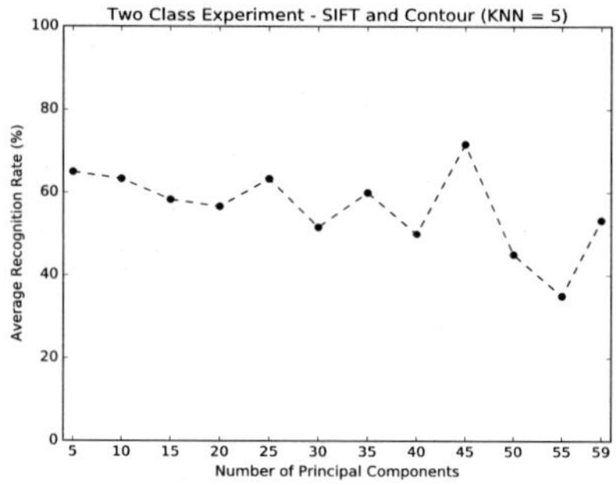

(a)

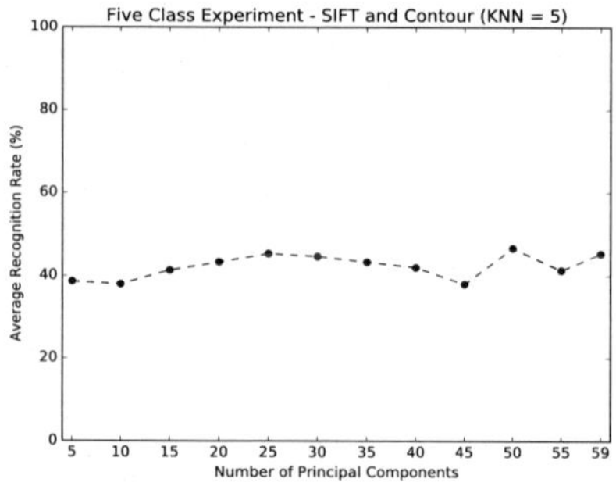

(b)

Figure 14. Recognition rates of KNN ($K = 5$), boundary and SIFT key points, with LDA features and 6-fold cross validation. (a) Binary classification using classes 1 and 3 of Figure 4. (b) Five-class experiment.

Table 4. Minimum and maximum accuracies, denoted by $\min$ and $\max$, respectively, for two and five-classes test using SIFT and $K = 5$, in the PCA+DA space

g	$[\min, \max]$	n_{pca} for min	n_{pca} for max
2	$[35.0, 71.7]$	55	45
5	$[38.0, 46.7]$	10	50

Conclusion and Future Works

In this work, we explore graph features, computed through symmetric polynomials that are permutation invariants, in a statistical learning pipeline for static hand gesture recognition. The main stages of the proposed methodology are graph-cuts for hand segmentation, spectral features computation, dimensionality reduction through PCA, LDA projection, and KNN classification. With this approach we get suitable recognition rates (73.3%) for two class separating problems. However, for multi-class we noticed a performance degradation achieving maximum accuracy of 57.8% for $g = 3$, 59.2% if $g = 4$, and only 46.7% for $g = 5$. Besides, we have noticed problems in the graph-cuts segmentation when changing the illumination conditions.

In order to address the mentioned limitations, we shall consider a more robust classifier, like support vector machines [46], and apply deep learning techniques for human hand detection/segmentation [20]. Also, we must perform further works to improve the graph quality for hand pose representation. Besides, we must consider upper and lower bounds for the Laplacian eigenvalues of the graphs [47], as well as expressions (33)-(36), to analyze the results of Figure 10. Moreover, more experiments with SIFT replacing the skeleton must be undertaken to be sure about the strengths and weaknesses of SIFT for our methodology.

References

[1] Yao, Y. and Li, C-T. Hand gesture segmentation in uncontrolled environments with partition matrix and a spotting scheme based on hidden conditional random fields. In *Pattern Recognition (ACPR), 2013 2nd IAPR Asian Conference on*, pages 842–846, Nov 2013.

[2] Chaudhary, Ankit, Raheja, J.L., Das, Karen and Raheja, Sonia. A Survey on Hand Gesture Recognition in Context of Soft Computing. In Natarajan Meghanathan, BrajeshKumar Kaushik, and Dhinaharan Nagamalai, editors, *Advanced Computing*, volume 133 of *Communications in Computer and Information Science*, pages 46–55. Springer Berlin Heidelberg, 2011.

[3] Leite, Diego Augusto T. Q., Duarte, Julio C., Pereira Neves, Luiz Antônio, de Oliveira, Jauvane C. and Giraldi, Gilson A. Hand gesture recognition from depth and infrared kinect data for CAVE applications interaction. *Multimedia Tools Appl.*, 76(20):20423–20455, 2017.

[4] Mitra S. and Acharya, T. Gesture Recognition: A Survey. *Trans. Sys. Man Cyber Part C*, 37(3):311–324, May 2007.

[5] Rautaray Siddharth S. and Agrawal, Anupam. Vision based hand gesture recognition for human computer interaction: A survey. *Artif. Intell. Rev.*, 43(1):1–54, January 2015.

[6] Nagarajan, S. and Subashini, T.S. Image based hand gesture recognition using statistical features and soft computing techniques. *Int. Journal of Emerging Technology and Advanced Engineering*, 5(7):476–482, July 2015.

[7] Howe, Lim Wei Wong, F. and Chekima, A. Comparison of hand segmentation methodologies for hand gesture recognition. In *2008 International Symposium on Information Technology*, volume 2, pages 1–7, Aug 2008.

[8] Morerio, P. Marcenaro, L. and Regazzoni, C.S. Hand detection in first person vision. In *Proceedings of the 16th International Conference on Information Fusion*, pages 1502–1507, July 2013.

[9] Xie S. and Pan, J. Hand detection using robust color correction and gaussian mixture model. In *2011 Sixth International Conference on Image and Graphics*, pages 553–557, Aug 2011.

[10] Li, Yin, Sun, Jian, Tang, Chi-Keung and Shum, Heung-Yeung. Lazy snapping. *ACM Trans. Graph.*, 23(3):303–308, August 2004.

[11] Zhou, T., Ruan, Q., Wan, J., and An, G. Embedded accelerated gaussian model in graph cuts for automatic hand segmentation. In *2013 IEEE International Conference on Signal Processing, Communication and Computing (ICSPCC 2013)*, pages 1–6, Aug 2013.

[12] Triesch, Jochen and von der Malsburg, Christoph. Classification of hand postures against complex backgrounds using elastic graph matching. *Image Vision Comput.*, 20(13-14):937–943, 2002.

[13] Viola, Paul and Jones, Michael J. Robust real-time face detection. *Int. J. Comput. Vision*, 57(2):137–154, May 2004.

[14] Yun, L. and Peng, Z. An automatic hand gesture recognition system based on viola-jones method and svms. In *2009 Second International Workshop on Computer Science and Engineering*, volume 2, pages 72–76, Oct 2009.

[15] Jadwaa, S.K. Feature Extraction for Hand Gesture Recognition: A Review. *Int. Journal of Scientific & Engineering Research*, 6(7), July 2015.

[16] Hasan, Mokhtar M. and Mishra, Pramod K. Hand gesture modeling and recognition using geometric features: A review. *Canadian Journal on Image Processing and Computer Vision*, 3(1):12–26, March 2012.

[17] Chang, Chin-Chen, Chen, Jiann-Jone, Tai, Wen-Kai and Han, Chin-Chuan. New approach for static gesture recognition. *J. Inf. Sci. Eng.*, 22:1047–1057, 2006.

[18] Cheng, H. Yang, L. and Liu, Z. Survey on 3d hand gesture recognition. *IEEE Trans. on Circuits and Systems for Video Technology*, 26(9):1659–1673, Sept 2016.

[19] Chen, T.Y. Wu, M.Y., Hsieh, Y.H. and Fu, L.C. Deep learning for integrated hand detection and pose estimation. In *2016 23rd International Conference on Pattern Recognition (ICPR)*, pages 615–620, Dec 2016.

[20] Boyali, John, V., Mita, A., Imanishi, S.M. and Sanma, N. Deep learning-based fast hand gesture recognition using representative frames. In *2016 International Conference on Digital Image Computing: Techniques and Applications (DICTA)*, pages 1–8, Nov 2016.

[21] Lattari, L.G., Montenegro, A.A., Conci, A., Clua, E.G.W., Mota, V.F., Vieira, M.B. and Lizarraga, G. Using graph cuts in gpus for color based human skin segmentation. *Integrated Computer-Aided Enginnering*, 18(3):41–59, 2011.

[22] Lowe, David G. Distinctive Image Features from Scale-Invariant Keypoints. *Int. J. Comput. Vision*, 60(2):91–110, November 2004.

[23] Wilson, Richard C. Hancock, Edwin R. and Luo, Bin. Pattern vectors from algebraic graph theory. *IEEE Trans. Pattern Anal. Mach. Intell.*, 27(7):1112–1124, 2005.

[24] Cunningham, John P. and Ghahramani, Zoubin. Linear dimensionality reduction: Survey, insights, and generalizations. *J. of Mach. Learn. Research*, 16:2859–2900, 2015.

[25] Hastie, T., Tibshirani, R. and Friedman, J.H. *The Elements of Statistical Learning*. Springer, 2001.

[26] Giraldi, G.A. Rodrigues, P.S. Kitani, E.C. and Thomaz, C.E. Dimensionality reduction, classification and reconstruction problems in statistical learning approaches. *Revista de Informatica Teorica e Aplicada (RITA)*, 15(1):141–173, 2008.

[27] Boykov, Y. and Jolly, M.P. Interactive graph cuts for optimal boundary and region segmentation of objects in n-d images. *Proc. IEEE Int. Conf. on Computer Vision*, 2001.

[28] Li, Yin, Sun, Jian, Tang, Chi-Keung and Shum, Heung-Yeung. Lazy snapping. *ACM Trans. Graph.*, 23(3):303–308, 2004.

[29] Rother, Carsten Kolmogorov, Vladimir and Blake, Andrew. Grabcut: Interactive foreground extraction using iterated graph cuts. *ACM Transactions on Graphics*, 23:309–314, 2004.

[30] Gonzalez, R.C. and Woods, R.E. *Digital Image Processing*. Addison Wesley, 1992.

[31] Cvetković, D.M., Doob, M. and Sachs, H. *Spectra of Graphs: Theory and Application*. Deutscher Verlag der Wissenschaften.

[32] Beineke, L.W. and Wilson, R.J. *Topics in Algebraic Graph Theory*. Encyclopedia of Mathematics and Its Applications. Cambridge University Press, 2004.

[33] Carmichael, R.D. Review: L. E. Dickson, Elementary Theory of Equations. *Bull. Amer. Math. Soc.*, 21(5):247–249, 02 1915.

[34] Labbi, Mohammed Larbi and Labbi, M.L. *On some algebraic identities and the exterior product of double forms*. 2014.

[35] Garrett, Paul. Girard-Newton identities for symmetric functions. *Technical report*, University of Minnesota, January 2010.

[36] Maragos, P.A. and Schafer, R.W. Morphological Skeleton Representation and Coding of Binary Images. *IEEE Trans. Acoust., Speech, Signal Processing*, 34:1228–1244, Oct 1986.

[37] Sirovich, L. Low-dimensional procedure for the characterization of human faces. *Journal of Optical Society of America*, 4(3):519–524, 1987.

[38] Swets, D. and Weng, J. Using discriminants eigenfeatures for image retrieval. *IEEE Trans. Patterns Anal. Mach Intell.*, 18(8):831–836, 1996.

[39] Devijver, P.A. and Kittler, J. *Pattern Classification: A Statistical Approach*. Prentice-Hall, 1982.

[40] Fukunaga, K. *Introduction to Statistical Pattern Recognition*. Academic Press, New York, 1990.

[41] Zhu, M. and Hastie, T. J. Feature extraction for nonparametric discriminant analysis. *Journal of Computational and Graphical Statistics*, 12:101–120, 2003.

[42] Pisharady, Pramod and Saerbeck, Martin. *Recent methods and databases in vision-based hand gesture recognition: A review.* 141:152–165, 12 2015.

[43] Kim, Tae-Kyun, Wong, Shu-Fai and Cipolla, Roberto. Tensor canonical correlation analysis for action classification. In *CVPR*. IEEE Computer Society, 2007.

[44] Mohar, Bojan. The laplacian eigenvalues of graphs: a survey. *Discrete Mathematics*, 109(1):171 – 183, 1992.

[45] Boykov, Yuri. Computing geodesics and minimal surfaces via graph cuts. In *International Conference on Computer Vision*, pages 26–33, 2003.

[46] Vapnik, Vladimir N. *Statistical Learning Theory*. John Wiley & Sons, INC., 1998.

[47] Zhang, X.-D. The Laplacian eigenvalues of graphs: a survey. *ArXiv e-prints*, November 2011.

In: Gesture Recognition
Editors: G. Coleman and R. Ward
ISBN: 978-1-53613-491-9

Chapter 4

Identification of Pointing and Waving in Gesture-Based Human-Machine-Interaction

***Tobias Nowack*[*], *Peter Kurtz*[†] and *Hartmut Witte*[‡]**
Fakultät für Maschinenbau,
Technische Universität Ilmenau, Germany

Abstract

To make use of gesture detection in HMI, algorithms for their occurrence in working processes should be defined. Since affordable motion capturing devices like Microsoft® Kinect® in science and industry were proved to be simply applicable in working environments, we developed and studied the functionality of two algorithms for the detection of pointing gestures, and one approach for waving on this technological base.

The "phase model" of speech supporting gestures by McNeill (1992) proposes to structure a gesture into three (optional five) phases. This phase model is the base of a technical description, which can be shown to be able to automatically detect "pointing" and "waving."

[*] Corresponding Author: Tobias.Nowack@tu-ilmenau.de.
[†] Corresponding Author: Peter.Kurtz@tu-ilmenau.de.
[‡] Corresponding Author: Hartmut.Witte@tu-ilmenau.de.

Differing static and dynamic gestures, detection rates are up to 85%, if the interacting human turns less than 30° in relation to the frontal aspect of the MS® Kinect® sensor. In pointing gestures "static" was identified to mean that the body posture should be kept for about 0.5 seconds. If the pointing algorithm rejects a gesture as "not pointing," the motion is checked for resembling "waving." "Waving" is characterized by a dynamic (periodic) stroke phase which may be detected by a frequency analysis (FFT), without any necessity of keeping positions.

At the present state, having analyzed 1073 recorded gesture sequences, the "static pointing algorithm" provides a detection rate of about 53%, the "phase-based approach for pointing" a detection rate of about 86%, and the "waving algorithm" a detection rate of about 82%. In a parallel project, in structured environment algorithms for pointing reached 92% detection rate using stochastic approaches. But this strategy turned out to be very sensitive to changes of the environment, while the above described deterministic approaches proved to be rather robust. Whether a combination of both strategies improves and stabilizes detection rates, is under study.

Keywords: gesture, pointing, waving

1. Introduction

Since 2010 affordable motion capturing devices (e.g., MS® Kinect®) are available. They primarily have been developed for gaming purposes. However, shortly after introduction to the market, those systems also have been established for analyses of Human-Machine-Interaction (HMI). One of the first commercial deployments has been a system introduced by Fraunhofer IOSB and BMW (Schick & Sauer, 2013). They made use of the MS® Kinect® sensor to detect a worker pointing to a failure on a painted surface. As these devices are cheap, and the postprocessing algorithms are quite robust in unknown environments, they are well suited for interactions with mobile systems.

Humans normally use gesture speech to support oral communication. McNeill (1992) identified, that gestures may be divided into four to five different categories. Not all categories of speech-attended gestures may be used for HMI purposes.

The usability of a product, which includes its HMI, may be described following DIN 9241-11 (1999) within the context of its use. Consecutively, the use of gestures has to work in different ways, like we generally use gestures in human communication with changing information content.

For example, to localize any kind of object in human-to-human communication, we support our speech by a pointing gesture. If humans interact in environments provoking e.g., by noise special requirements, silent gestures have to substitute speech in case of commanding. One example for a commanding gesture is waving. If somebody is asked to wave, without defining the context of commanding, most experimentees intuitively will use waving in a social context to code "Hello!" or "Good bye!" - beckoning. "A wave is a nonverbal communication gesture that consists of the movement of the hand and/or entire arm that people commonly use to greet each other but can also be used to say goodbye" (this definition seems to be generally acceptable, since it is given in (Wikipedia, "Wave," 2017).

In this contribution, the term "waving" is used in analogy to "semaphoring" or "signalizing" solemnly using arms and hands – thus in the following we take reference to communication theory with emphasis on signal theory.

2. Human to Human Communication with Gestures

2.1. Gestures

"A gesture is a form of non-verbal communication or non-vocal communication in which visible bodily actions communicate particular messages, either in place of, or in conjunction with, speech." (Wikipedia, Gesture, 2017, citing in modified form Kendon, 2004).

This definition explains that gestures as non-verbal communication support verbal communication, for example as the pointing gesture supports the localization of something. To point somewhere in the field of view is usually much easier than to describe the position. If you must localize a file in a bookshelf, you can point onto and say, “pick up the file over there,” or if you only localize with speech you must specify the position like “the third file from the left in the second shelf next to the door on the third board from the top.”

Waving is used instead of speech, if a human does command somebody to come over. This might be the best way to communicate if verbal communication is not possible because of noise or perhaps windows.

Even the use of pointing instead of verbal communication makes sense, if verbal communication is impossible. As McNeill (1992) described in his observation, a 12-month aged child already used pointing to communicate with its parents. The “child reaches out in the direction of a desired object, and looks away from the object and to the adult who is in a different direction. Such a gesture could still be in part reaching, but the child clearly includes the adult in a communicative loop with the gesture” (McNeill, 1992, p. 300).

2.2. Communication

Communication described technically by Shannon & Weaver (1964) basically is a one-way process (Figure 1). The “information source” as a “sender” codes his information as a “message,” which will be transmitted as a “signal” via a “channel.” This channel may be disturbed by “noise” originating from a wide variety of possible “noise sources.” The process of receiving will be the other way around, the “receiver” will copy the signal, reconstruct the message, which best should be decoded to the same information reaching the “destination” (Figure 1).

In this technical system view, the influences of human aspects are not included. The sender as well as the receiver have their own basic knowledge, their own cultural background, and their personal (individual) way to code information. At a first glance, the cultural background is expressed by the language. The sender e.g., codes the information in English, the receiver only can decode German - the communication by words will not work. Another example of cultural background is the gesture coding for yes and no. In most western countries "Yes" will be coded as moving the head forward and backward (nodding), whereas "No" will be coded as turning the head left/right (head shaking). In northern Greece and Bulgaria, the gesture of cradling the head left / right will be agreement, whereas throwing the head backwards will mean disagreement (Lohrmann, 2017).

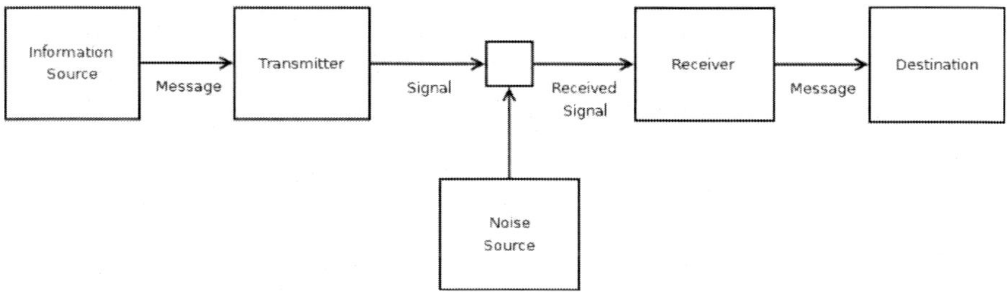

Figure 1. Communication model by Shannon and Weaver (Shannon & Weaver, 1964, p. 7).

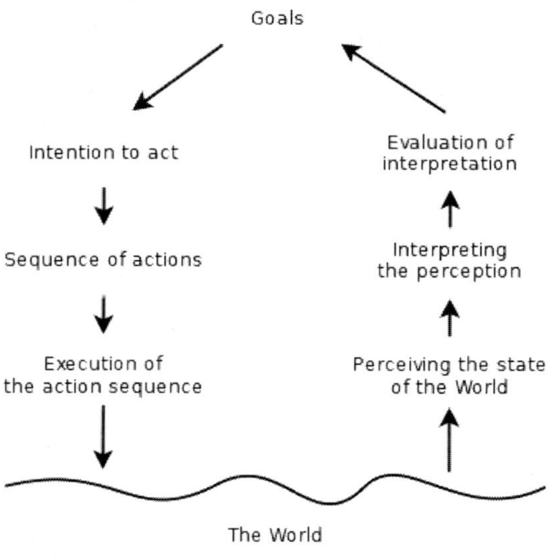

Figure 2. Seven Stages of Action (Norman, 1988/2002, p. 47).

At the end, human communication will not only work in one direction as commanding, it works like a cycle process. One communication partner sends the information and checks, if the other partner receives the information. If both think the information exchanged is the same, communication continues, and the sender will proof the change of the world by the receiver as described in the model of Donald Norman (Figure 2). If the receiving person is not sure to have decoded the correct information, it will request this information, for example by coding it with own words, and answer with those (backward message). The primary sender now may confirm or correct the information.

2.3. Context

To support communication, human beings make use of additional knowledge to decode the information from the message. If this "context" of the communication is common to the interaction partners (e.g., to refer to a "box"), and one partner points into a specific direction, the other already understands the request to look over there and to search for any kind of a box. With support of this additional "context knowledge," gesture communication enables the use of unprecise pointing. The cognitive human potential allows combining the different information channels to achieve a possible goal in an optimized manner.

In research on waving it has to be taken into account, that and how this effect also influences the way of performing the waving gesture. There are two main understandings of waving:

1. waving to command "Come over!" – "semaphoring" or "signalizing"
2. waving to communicate "Hello!" or "Good bye!" – "beckoning."

In the studies presented here, the experimentees were intrigued to perform gestures "intuitively," as they understand the demand to wave. The instructor only introduced the recording of the movement, and that the characteristic movement during performance of the gesture was identifiable by a human. To record uninfluenced movements each experimentee could perform the gesture for a given command as "Point with the right hand!" or "Wave with the right hand!". As the experimentees did not have any context knowledge, for example that the waving should command a robot or a driver in his car, most experimentees used the way to wave right - left with the forearm or the hand in the basic version of starting or stopping a communication.

DIN ISO 9241-11 already provides a special look onto the context, within the definition of usability measurement. Usability criteria ("effectiveness," "efficiency" and "satisfaction") only may be measured for a special user group in a special context.

2.4. Acceptance – Intuitiveness

If the context and the user group are unprecisely defined or unknown, as it was during the experiments, it is difficult to identify / measure usability. The parameters "effectiveness" (accuracy and completeness by which users achieve specified goals) and "efficiency" (resources used in relation to the results achieved) in case of a technical solution could be measured by the "recognition rate."

The parameter "satisfaction" (person's perceptions and responses that result from the use of a system, product or service) in our experimental setup is not measurable. Satisfaction is an individual parameter which must be measured in the context of use via communication with the potential user. In our test setup, this question will be reversely processed. The experimentees have been asked to perform the gestures as they would prefer it without feeling annoyed. As described above, the investigator only gave commands without forcing a special body movement. By this setup, the experimentees should perform intuitive gestures, which they accepted themselves.

Additionally, the acceptance is dominated by the response time of a technical system. Herczeg (2009) discusses that repetitive use of a technical system generates expectations about the interaction behavior. A response time of about 3 up to 4 seconds is hypothetized to be the best, otherwise the error rate increases and the number of errors is stated to be reciprocal to the grade of acceptance.

In our study, "error rate" and "handling time" are estimates for measures of acceptance.

3. Model of Gestures

3.1. Classification

There are various theoretical approaches to classify gestures. The first idea has been a classification by the way how to translate a command into a gesture. There are gestures which try to "command" the communication partner to do something. This command here is called "dynamic command," since it is performed with a dynamic gesture – e.g., the command "Come over!," which will be performed as forward and backward waving of the hand/forearm. A "dynamic command" forces the recipient to perform any kind of motion like "walking," "lifting good" or "assemble units"; all processes where the body or parts of the body are in action.

On the other hand, "static commands" are performed within a fixed body posture, only one segment of the motor apparatus does perform gross motion. A "static command" is a command which forces to finish an action (e.g., stay) or which is needed to define a static object (e.g., pointing). As a typical example the pointing gesture is described in the following chapter. "Pointing" is relative to a body posture. It may indicate any direction to the communication partner. As described in the last chapter, pointing is a supporting gesture in human to human communication. To specify the meaning of the gesture, additional (context) knowledge is necessary. Comparable behavior may be described for other static gestures, e.g., the stop gesture. This gesture is used to stop a body movement. In this case, the gesture should as well be static, meaning: "Stop your movement and stay static!"

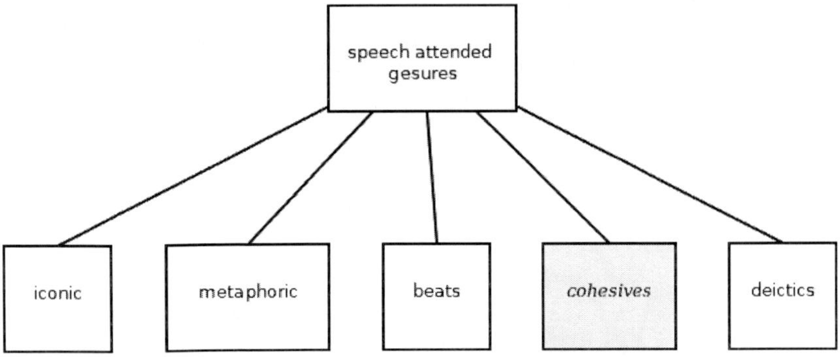

Figure 3. Classification of "speech attended gestures" by McNeill (1992).

3.2. Gesture Space

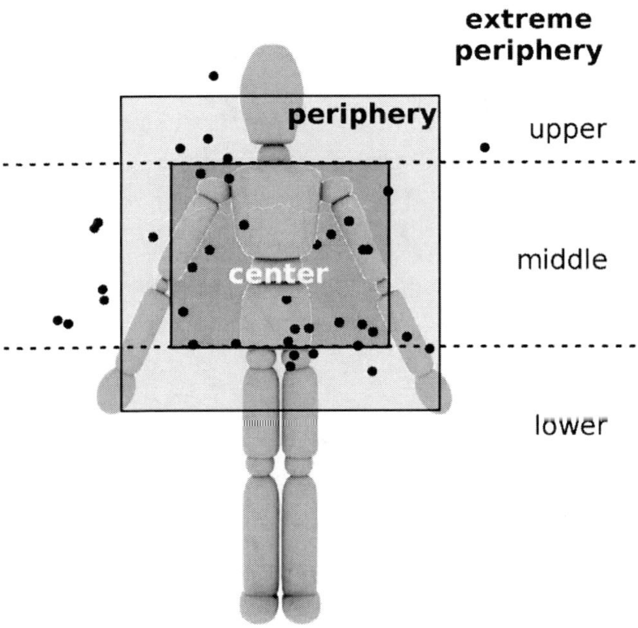

Figure 4. Typical gesture space of deictic gestures (modified by Stefan Jehring and Danja Voges according to a figure of McNeill 1992, p. 91).

During his analyses McNeill identified that gestures are performed "as shallow disk in front of the speaker, the bottom half flattened when the

Another classification has been developed by McNeill (199 This author describes five classes (mostly only four of them are used, s Figure 3). He classifies "speech attended gestures," gestures that or support speech and do not have an individual meaning.

One class, the "beat gestures" do not support the speech directly, th support the orator to be in sync with the rhythm of speech. This class gesturers is not applicable to commanding gestures, it is not necessary identify these gestures by technical recognition systems.

The behavior of "iconic" or "metaphoric" gestures is to illustrate th content of speech. The main difference is that iconic gestures make use c predefined icons. These might be icons, which are predefined for specia groups like divers or soldiers, which have their own sign language in thei special environment and thus context. On the other hand, there ar metaphoric gestures, which use abstract metaphoric interpretations of th speech context. To understand the metaphoric gestures, additiona (context) knowledge is necessary. "Metaphoric" is the individual interpretation of speech content. To understand the problem of decoding of a metaphoric gesture, we must have a look onto the communication model by Shannon (cp. Figure 1). The person performing the gesture uses own interpretation of the information to code it into a gesture message. The communication partner, another person or a technical system, needs to know about the same code, requires the same knowledge background to decode the gesture message into the same command as the sender.

The fourth type of gestures are "deictic." The pointing gesture is the main deictic gesture. *"Pointing has the obvious function of indicating objects and events in the concrete world, but also plays a part even where there is nothing objectively present to point at."* (McNeill, 1992, p. 18). Following the gesture classification for human-machine-interaction proposed by McNeill, it seems to be best to primarily make use of iconic or deictic gestures.

speaker is seated […]. Adults usually perform gestures within this limited space (with children the space is larger" (McNeill 1992, p. 86). As he separated the gesture space into the areas projected on a frontal plane named "center," "periphery" and "extreme periphery," he could identify that different classes of gestures are performed in those different areas. "Iconic" gestures are performed in the "center," while "deictic" gestures tend to be performed in the "periphery" (Figure 4).

3.3. General Phase Model

All kind of body movements may always be separated into series of short basic motions. In general they are called "preparation," "stroke" and "recovery" (Meinel & Schnabel, 2015). Based on the concept of these three phases, Kendon (2004) describes a "gesture unit." In his idea, only the first two parts "preparation" and "stroke" are necessary to code the content of a gesture, and he defines this combination to be a "gesture phase" (see Figure 5). This model is comparable to the model of McNeill (1992). Both describe the intuitively performed, speech attended gesture. But McNeill adds two additional, but optional "holds", the "pre- and post-stroke hold." Speech attended gestures have to be in sync with the speech. Thus, "preparation" is the time to move the hand into gesture space, to move directly to the starting point of stroke phase. The main phase (stroke phase) should start synchronously with the content of speech, thus the orator must synchronize both.

Several gestures finish with a body posture that is used to emphasize the current content; e.g., the attention gesture or the pointing gesture indicate to the selected destination. This emphasizing is timed during the post-stroke hold.

Here, the phase model is enhanced for use in the HMI context. In the special HMI task addressed, context gestures should be used without the recognition of speech, they perhaps will be used in circumstances where other interaction forms are disadvantageous. On this way, the gesture must be technically detectable without additional information.

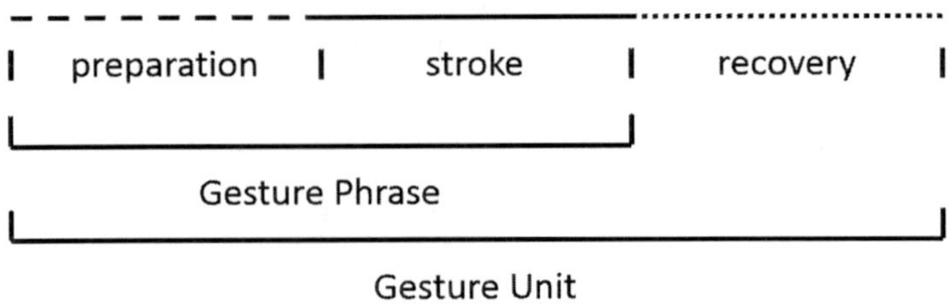

Figure 5. Phase of gestures following Kendon (2004).

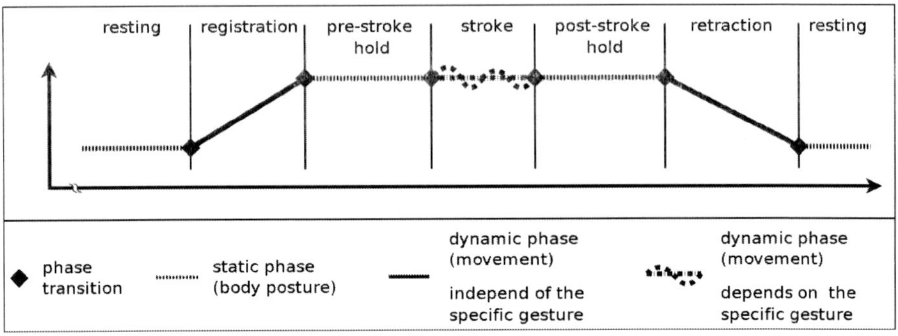

Figure 6. Phase definition for technical gesture detection (Nowack, 2017).

Figure 6 illustrates the general idea to divide a gesture into 7 phases. Phase 1 and 7 are equivalent and represent the "resting" phase(s). The "preparation" or "registration" phase starts the gesture sequence. "Pre-stroke hold" is followed by a mandatory "stroke" phase, which might be finished by a "post-stroke hold." The gesture sequence concludes with the "termination" phase. Most phases, excluding resting and stroke phase, are optional and define the different gestures individually.

3.4. Pointing

As already has been described, the main information of pointing is (de-)coded during the "post-stroke hold" by the pointing vector – which indicates the destination. In human to human communication this information is presented by the sender, and the receiver will try to identify the destination object the sender points on. The way the receiver reads /

decodes the pointing is individual and will be recognized in feedback by the sender. When the sender mentions that the receiver identified the destination object, "termination" phase is entered.

If a technical system has to recognize the "post-stroke hold", other parameters must be identified. In our attempt, the cycle process of communication between the communication partners is not implemented right now.

3.5. Waving

Apart from the above given differentiation of "beckoning" and "semaphoring," in the latter sense the term "waving" may have different meanings.

The use of waving as a commanding gesture in more technical environments, e.g., helping drivers during entering their parking position, is another meaning of this gesture. Having a closer technical look on the motion of hand/forearm, only the spatial orientation of the movement will primarily be different. Whereas the communication gesture "Hello!" or "Good bye!" describes a movement from left to right, the commanding gesture "Come over!" or "Go away"/"push backwards!" will be realized as movement forward – backward.

The main difference in the phase model between the more static pointing gesture and the dynamic waving gesture is, that waving will precise in the stroke phase, whereas pointing is finished after the "post stroke hold" by the occurence of a "release."

4. Technical Description

4.1. Technical Sensor

For our work we decided to use cheap consumable technical sensors like MS® Kinect®. There are several advantages of these kinds of sensors.

The main advantage is the low price. With about 200 € the MS® Kinect® 2 Sensor is simply affordable for different fields of application. One can integrate such a sensor into a mobile robotic system as well as setup several sensors in the environment, if used it in house automation.

This kind of sensors, developed for gaming, is rather robust against changing environmental visual conditions. Integrated algorithms work in different surroundings without the need of long time for calibration, since the basic use in gaming does not allow long time for setup. The sensor and the available libraries must detect a person in front of the sensor without additional markers on the clothes.

The advantage of the availability of libraries is combined fix with the disadvantage of unknown algorithms underlying body detection and motion analysis. The position of the "skeletal joints" is more erroneous than in a marker based system.

A cheap system connected via USB-3 and software libraries is rather limited in its data bandwidth. The framerate in practice is only 30 frames per second (fps) instead of a high-quality system like Qualisys® or Vicon® with capture rates of 120 fps to 2.000 fps.

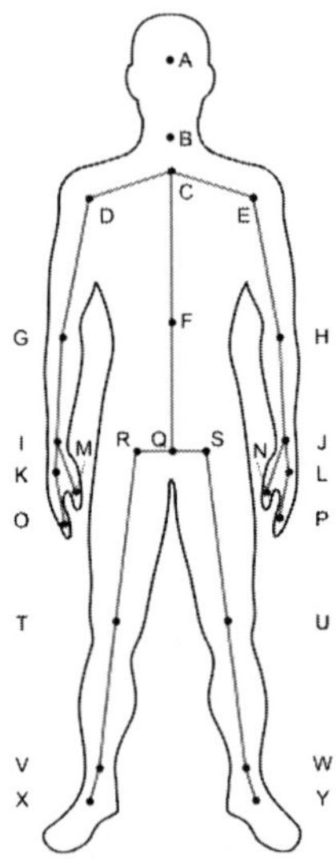

A	Head
B	Neck
C	Spine shoulder
D/E	Shoulder
F	Spine mid
G/H	Elbow
I/J	Wrist
K/L	Hand
M/N	Thumb tip
O/P	Finger tip (Hand tip)
Q	Spine base
R/S	Hip
T/U	Knee
V/W	Ankle
X/Y	Foot

Figure 7. Stick figure with skeleton joints according to the definition for MS® Kinect®.V2

For development and examination, the algorithms provided by Microsoft® detect 25 "skeleton joints" (Figure 7). Even if only skeleton joints "hip and above" are used for analyses, it is necessary that the human being is completely visible in the field of view.

4.2. Basic Model

The basic model of detecting a gesture has already been described in the last chapter (see Figure 6). As a computer needs algorithms to separate the different phases defined above, events have to be identified, indicating change of phase. These events are described by threshold values of kinematic parameters.

The algorithm developed has to work stable, independent of user (body size, face color or hair length), environment (indoor, outdoor, sun, light) or the motion caption system (here MS® Kinect®). These reasons force to find parameters, which could be derived from the given skeleton joint data. Most skeleton joints are connected via "bones." Angles between these bones can be calculated independent of all influences mentioned.

The parameter to define the phases are calculated from the change or value of an angle and the duration of this change. The events between two phases e.g., are changes in angle velocity, for example when the gesture starts, between "resting phase" and "registration." Here the basic parameter is the shoulder angle, which must overcome 20°, while the angular velocity at this event is higher than 1° per frame.

4.3. Parameter for Pointing Detection

The most interesting angle to detect pointing is the shoulder angle. The "shoulder joint" given by MS® Kinect® has no exact anatomical equivalent, and connects a virtual "arm" vector (Hand – Shoulder, $\overline{HS}$) with a referenze vector "torso" ($\bar{T}$), which is referred to the "spine" (spine-base – spine shoulder).

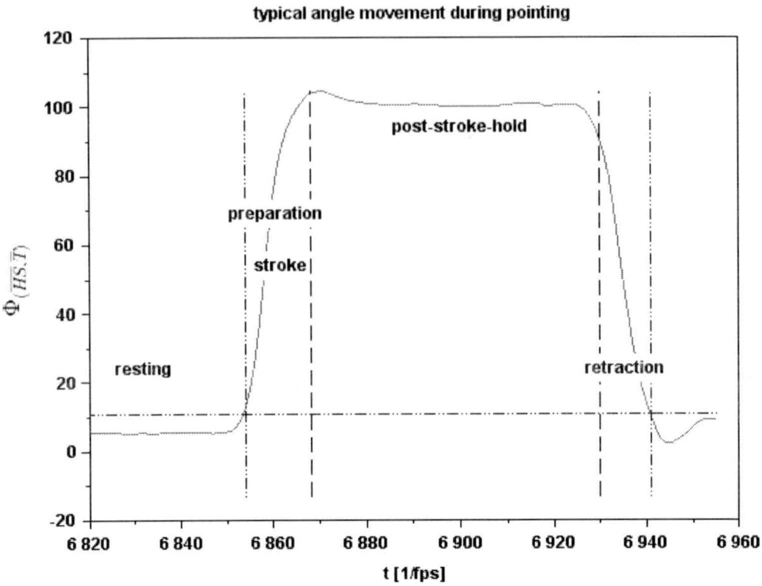

Figure 8. Typical angular movement during pointing.

Sometimes pointing better is defined by the stretch of elbow, elbow joint angle > 160°. The arm is lifted out of the resting position (shoulder angle > 20°). The resting position is defined as arms hanging on the body, the shoulder angle $\Phi_{(\overline{HS},\overline{T})} < 20°$. If the arm is parallel to the torso the angle between the vector hand – shoulder and spine-base – spine-shoulder should be 0°. The joint detection system as well as the body itself is not as exact, that parallel must be defined as less than 20°.

So the arm leaves the resting position if the shoulder angle is > 20°. This body posture has to be kept for 0.5 s (Nowack et al., 2017). This algorithm does not detect if somebody is pointing with flexed arm and directed by the index finger.

Figure 8 shows a typical angle change for a pointing gesture. The experimentees always started in resting position, hands by side of the body. Because the pointing information is directed by body posture during post-stroke-hold, for pointing the preparation and the stroke phase are combined in a short movement directly starting from the resting position. The post-stroke-hold is characterized by an immobility during the holding period.

Immobility in case of a pointing arm means that angle velocity in the shoulder joint is below 1°/frame.

$$\left|\dot{\Phi}_{(\overline{HS},\bar{T})}\right| \leq \frac{1°}{frame} \quad (1)$$
$$\text{for } t \geq 6\, frames$$

Equation 1. Immobility during post-stroke-hold.

This immobility must be kept for at least 6 frames' duration. At the end of post-stroke-hold, retraction to the resting position starts. If another movement starts after the algorithm detects a post-stroke-hold, it is not registered to be a post-stroke-hold. In some cases, the movement fragment might be a pre-stroke-hold, before the stroke phase of another gesture will be performed. The retraction phase for the pointing gesture is described as a continuous movement back to the resting position, thus the angle velocity will be less than 0 °/frame.

$$\dot{\Phi}_{(\overline{HS},\bar{T})} \leq \frac{0°}{frame} \quad (2)$$
$$\text{until } \Phi_{(\overline{HS},\bar{T})} < 20\,°$$

Equation 2. Movement during retraction phase (pointing gesture)

4.4. Parameter for Waving Detection

The waving gesture could be described as an undulation. Mainly the forearm is moved, so the most interesting angle is the elbow joint angle. This angle is included by a virtual "forearm" (vector Elbow - Fingertip – $\overline{EFt}$) and the "upper arm" (Elbow – Shoulder - $\overline{ES}$).

Next it should be verified, if it is feasible to use the general model (see Figure 6) to detect the dynamic gesture waving as well. Instead of pointing, for waving the main information is coded by the movement of the arm, not by its final static position.

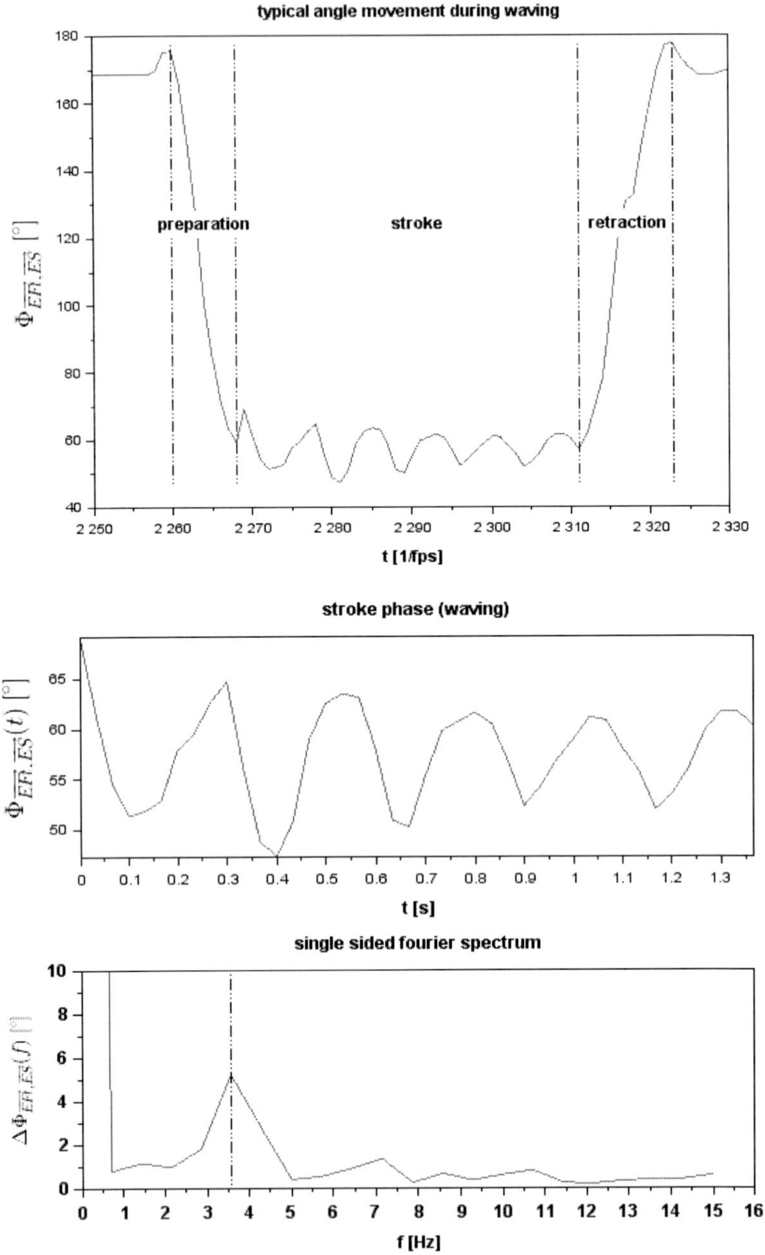

Figure 9. a) Typical angle movement during waving; b) Extracted stroke sequence and single sided Fourier spectrum.

Figure 9a shows that the typical angle movement during waving has a shape nearly similar to that of pointing. In the resting position, the arms are alongside the body, the elbow is stretched (elbow angle > 160°). During preparation phase the experimentees flexet the elbow to less than 130° and start with repetitive flexing of the elbow.

This repetitive flexing characterizes waving and may be described by the frequency of the alternating signal. As shown in Figure *9* b), this alternating signal has a frequency between 0.85 Hz and 6.7 Hz, with a minimum alternating angle $\Delta\Phi_{(\overline{EFt},\overline{ES})}$ higher than 3.1°.

$$\begin{aligned} &0.85\,Hz < f < 6.7\,Hz \\ &\text{with } \Delta\Phi_{(\overline{EFt},\overline{ES})} > 3.1° \end{aligned} \tag{3}$$

Equation 3. Threshold values to characterize stroke phase during waving.

5. Experiment and Result

To test the phase definition for technical gesture recognition, two experiments were designed. The experimentees in all experiments were placed in front of the MS® Kinect® System, facing towards the camera. The distance chosen allowed the MS® Kinect® device to watch all parts of the body necessary for whole body detection (the upper body as well as the thigh) during all phases of motion. The distance realized was in the range of 1.5 m to 3.0 m.

5.1. Pointing Experiments

The first experiments were designed to test the model of pointing. The experimentees were introduced to perform gestures, as in forcing a communication partner to recognize a given commands. Additionally, they got the information that the gestures performed should start and finish in the resting area, arms beside the body. They did not get any information about the methods of measurement.

Each experimentee should perform gestures in two different parts. In part one the investigator gave the command ("Point!" / "Wave!") and named the body side ("Right side!"/"Left side!"). For part two the investigator could address different marked points inside the laboratory. He asked the experimentee to point onto these points as well as to perform some control gestures, which should be rejected by the recognition algorithm. The sequence was: four times pointing, clapping, two times pointing, pointing onto the person of the experimentee itself, three times pointing and waving "Good bye!". The investigator decided, which target to use. Boundary condition was to force right- and left-handed pointing as well as pointing upward tilt to the ceiling or downward tilt to the floor.

MS® Kinect® software allows to record the joints' kinematic data as well as to provide colored stick figures. The sequences were manually coded for evaluation as following: the experimentee pointing right (ZR), left (ZL), waving to say: "Good bye!" (WR/WL), waving to command "Come over!" (HR/HL). All other gestures were called "control gestures" and coded (KR/KL). This manual coding was compared to the results of the detection algorithm. Those results then were classified into "true positive" (investigated gesture detected and performed), "true negative" (investigated gesture refused and not performed), "false positive" (investigated gesture detected but not performed) and "false negative" (investigated gesture refused but performed).

The overall result, called "Detection Rate", was calculated as the sum of true detections divided by the number of all sequences analyzed.

$$Detection\ Rate = \frac{\sum TP+TN}{\sum TP+TN+FP+FN} \tag{4}$$

Equation 4. Definition of Detection Rate.

For 302 gesture sequences analyzed, the detection rate of the first experiment was 85.4%. In the second experiment to develop the phase definition for waving, 771 gesture sequences analyzed led to a detection rate of 87.4%. The amount of pointing gestures during the first experiment was 55%, whereas the amount of pointing gestures in the second was 26%. Subsuming all experiments, 1073 gesture sequences were investigated. 370 gestures were identified to be pointing gestures, and the overall detection rate with the phase based algorithm to detect pointing was 86.9%.

The alternate algorithm identifying pointing only in the post stroke hold, not regarding the whole gesture sequence, detected just 169 pointing gestures correctly. The overall detection rate with this "static" algorithm was 53%. Advantages gainable for this algorithm are discussed in the chapter "Outlook."

5.2. Waving Experiment

The experiment has been divided into three parts. During part one, the experimentees should perform the gesture for a given command, as they liked to do. There was an equal command sequence for all three parts containing the commands "Wave!" / "Point!," and the information to perform right-handed or left-handed. As control the commands and consecutive sequences "Point upward!" or "Bowling!" were chosen. In the second part, the experimentees additionally got the information to perform the more technical version of waving in case of commanding "Come over!" or to perform the more communicational version, in case of "Say hello!" or "Say good bye!." During the last run of the experiment, the experimentees were introduced to perform waving in case of saying "Hello!" or "Good bye!".

The same four classes as above were applied for gaining detection rates. As already described above, the dataset for the waving detection algorithm contained 771 gesture sequences, including 541 (70%) sequences of waving. The recognition rate was 83.9%, after all parameters of the algorithm had been optimized. The optimized algorithm has been checked with the gesture sequences recorded during the pointing analyses. These 302 gestures sequences contained 76 (25%) waving sequences. The detection rate was 76.5%. Subsuming, the detection rate of waving for all 1073 gesture sequences is 81.8%.

6. Discussion

Based on ideas concerning the use of gestures which arose in linguistics and social sciences (Fricke, 2007), and combined with knowledge about biomechanics of human motion (Hochschild, 2005), the concept of the "phase model" of speech supporting gestures by McNeil (1992) is transferable to technical gesture recognition. Its simple implementation described here surprisingly provided gesture detection rates of more than 85%. Thus, it is possible to identify technically gestures by using the phase model and theoretically as well as experimentally identified threshold values for specified body angles.

In contrast to the results of own experiments with "pattern matching" recognition like those used in modern face recognition (which shall not be described here), the detection was lower (up to 87% vs. 92%), but the algorithms discussed here managed environmental changes rather robust, while the "pattern matching" recognition just failed. The detection rate of the "deterministic" approach based on the "phase model" of speech supporting gestures may be improved by systematic integration of context information, a strategy difficult to implement in "stochastic" approaches like pattern recognition. Not least, CPU time for the necessary algebraic calculation in deterministic approaches are much shorter than in stochastic ones, even when lookup tables are used. Those not awaited high detection rates gained with cheap technology (MS® Kinect®) in combination with a simple algebraic calculus make an application of the concept with specialized devices promising.

The experimental design allowed the experimentees to perform gestures as they would do it in their daily "human-human-communication." Forcing the experimentees to perform the gestures on their own perception of the command, various interpretations could be recorded. Even without additional knowledge of the human context (and in this case in contradiction to DIN EN ISO 9241-11) it was possible to reach detection rates above 80%.

In the data could be identified, that some experimentees perform pointing gestures with the complete right or the left arm, some only with the forearm and a few only with the index finger. Same behavior could be identified during the waving experiment. Most experimentees just used the hand. If the experimentees already know the MS® Kinect® sensor or got knowledge about the capability of the recording system, they used the forearm. As discussed in the theoretical chapter, the context including knowledge has large influences on the individual idea of performing a gesture.

6.1. Special Forms of Pointing

Pointing with both arms could also be seen in the recordings. In this case it is difficult to decide, which arm points to the mentioned target. Pointing with two arms can be performed in two different behaviors. Pointing with both arms towards one selected target might mention a kind of enhancement. The acting person tries to force the observer to follow its pointing vector. On the other hand, the acting person also can perform a sequence of pointing. The sequence and its meaning could be: first point onto the source object, second in the time line point onto the target object or place.

The first special form of pointing may be determined by the target vector, which points into the same orientation. To identify the meaning of the second form (pointing in sequence), additional detection mechanisms are necessary. For example, in one corresponding project, pointing should address transport boxes, the place to pick up and the place for release. In this project the recognition system "knew" that transport boxes had to be handled. If the system identified these objects it could decide, whether it is the object and place to pick up, or if there is an empty place with enough space to place and release the object transported.

6.2. Recognition Capability

The differently performed gestures of waving provoke the deficiencies of the recognition system. Waving in the behavior of "Hello!" or "Good bye!" are used in "nearfield" gesture communication. This means, the acting person performs waving with its hand. The affected joints are "fingertip," "thumb" or perhaps "hand" (see Figure 7). All these joints are very closely neighbored and could hardly be separated by the MS® Kinect® algorithms. The missing joints thus have to be interpolated.

A similar effect could be identified, when the body covered the arm while pointing onto any regular object. Humans may complete uncompleted outlines due to their individual knowledge. The technical device used didn't possess this capability. During the experiments, this problem appeared only if the user turned more than 60° to the side, relative to the line of sight.

6.3. Responsible User

The last question which has to be discussed here is the question for the "responsible user." During experiments in the laboratory were present: an experimentee, the investigator and an experiment leader. Only the experimentee was visible to the MS® Kinect®, and only this person performed the gestures. But if the algorithm is used outside the laboratory, there will be more than one person in front of the MS® Kinect®. As the MS® Kinect® V2 could decode the movement of up to six persons, a way to identify the "responsible user" (or "target person") is necessary. An easy solution perhaps could be an additional device to identify that responsible user. Realization ideas range from the use of some colored clothes to a special electronical device.

Conclusion and Outlook: Online System

Technical gesture detection may be improved by taking the user's individual concept of the meaning of gestures and their intuitive performance and reception into account: see here the kinematic differences between communication by "beckoning" and commanding by "waving." This concept may be applied to other kinds of gestures (taking cultural and social boundary conditions into account), making fuzzy limitation to standardized signalizing manageable by kinematic definition. Differently to the results of stochastic approaches, the outcome of deterministic approaches theoretically may reach detection rates up to 100%, depending on the degree of integration of relevant context information. Recognition systems that "understand" what is observed, need to own artificial intelligence. For sure, the largest challenge remains individuality in performance of movements.

The response time dominates the acceptance of interactive technical systems. As the algorithms need observation data of the whole sequence to detect whether it is pointing or waving, an online system has perceptible delay in recognition after the gesture finished. The human interaction partner has no opportunity to influence detection during the delay time, and the detection will probably fail. To increase the working speed, it has to be checked if both algorithms may work together in a two step-system. To speed up an online system, it will be necessary to support the human actor during performing the gesture. The system needs to indicate correct performance of each phase. This might not be easy, because the system has to "pre-predict" the gesture repeatedly during the first phases.

Right now, a workable alternative with the "static" algorithm is already in use for a system on a handling assistant robot. This algorithm detects pointing by three parameters only during "post-stroke hold." While the user performs the gesture in front of the robot, the algorithm indicates via light signs, if the body posture was interpretable, and that the system is waiting for acknowledgement after the holding time. As the acting person is more flexible, it is able to learn, how to perform correct pointing gestures to speed up the recognition system. A basic advantage of feedback integration beneath learning is the continuous cycling sequence of the seven states of actions defined by Norman (1988/2002), which allows the user to steadily react to changes of his environment.

Acknowledgments

We would like to express or special thanks *in memoriam* Danja Voges. Like in a multitude of preceding projects, we could take advantage of her skills and experiences in motion analysis as in graphical design. Christoph Dutschmann, Sabine Wenzel and Yue Xiong supported our work in different ways.

References

DIN EN ISO 9241-11, 1999, *Ergonomische Anforderungen für Bürotätigkeiten mit Bildschirmgeräten Teil 11: Anforderungen an die Gebrauchstauglichkeit* [*Ergonomic requirements for office work with VDUs Part 11: Performance requirements*] - Leitsätze, Berlin, Beuth Verlag ICS 13.180;35.080;35.180 (DIN EN ISO 9241-11).

Fricke, E., 2007, *Origo, Geste und Raum: Lokaldeixis im Deutschen* [*Origo, gesture and space: Lokaldeixis in German*], De Gruyter, Berlin, New York.

Herczeg, M., 2009, *Software-Ergonomie: Theorien, Modelle und Kriterien für gebrauchstaugliche interaktive Computersysteme* [*Software Ergonomics: theories, models and criteria for usable interactive computer systems*], 3rd edn., Oldenbourg, München.

Hochschild, J., 2005, *Grundlagen zur Wirbelsäule, HWS und Schädel, BWS und Brustkorb, obere Extremität* [*Basics of the spine, cervical spine and skull, thoracic and thorax, upper limb*], 3rd edn., Thieme, Stuttgart [u.a.].

Kendon, A., 2004, *Gesture: Visible action as utterance*, Cambridge University Press, Cambridge, New York.

Lohrmann, Julia, 2017, Ist das Kopfschütteln überall auf der Welt das Zeichen für "Nein" und das Nicken des Kopfes das Signal für "Ja"?, [The shaking of the head all over the world is the sign for no" and the nod of the head the signal for "Yes"?, *ARD,* viewed 7 Feb 2018, on https://www.planet-wissen.de/gesellschaft/kommunikation/koerpersprache/pwiewissensfrage156.html.

McNeill, D., 1995, ©1992, *Hand and mind: What gestures reveal about thought,* University of Chicago Press, Chicago.

Meinel, K. & Schnabel, G., 2015, *Bewegungslehre - Sportmotorik: Abriss einer Theorie der sportlichen Motorik unter pädagogischem Aspekt* [*Kinematics - sports motor skills: Demolition of a theory of sportive motor skills under pedagogical aspect*], 12th edn., Meyer et Meyer, Aachen.

Norman, D. A., 2002, ©1988, *The design of everyday things*, 1st edn., *Basic Books,* New York, from http://www.gbv.de/dms/bs/toc/507869923.pdf.

Nowack, T., 2017, *Mensch-Technik-Interaktion mittels Freiraumgesten',* Dissertationsschrift, Technische Universität Ilmenau [*Human-Technique Interaction via Free Space Gestures',* doctoral thesis,. Technical university Ilmenau].

Nowack, T., Lutherdt, S., Jehring, S., Xiong, Y., Wenzel, S. & Kurtz, P., 2017, 'Detecting Deictic Gestures for Control of Mobile Robots,' in P. Savage-Knepshield and J. Chen (eds.), *Advances in Human Factors in Robots and Unmanned Systems*, pp. 87–96.

Savage-Knepshield, P. & Chen, J. (eds.), 2017, *Advances in Human Factors in Robots and Unmanned Systems*, Springer International Publishing, Cham.

Schick, A. & Sauer, O., 2013, *Gestenbasierte Qualitätskontrolle: Intuitive Mensch-Maschine-Interaktion in der Industrie* [*Gesture-Based Quality Control: Intuitive human-machine interaction in the industry*], Düsseldorf, from http://www.iosb.fraunhofer.de/servlet/is/44590/Artikel%20Gesteninteraktion.pdf?command=downloadContent&filename=Artikel%20Gesteninteraktion.pdf.

Shannon, C. E. & Weaver, W., 1964 [©1949] *The mathematical theory of communication,* University of Illinois Press, Urbana.

Wikipedia, Gestures, 2017, *Gesture – Wikipedia, The Free Encyclopedia*, from https://en.wikipedia.org/w/index.php?title=Gesture&oldid=804225472.

Wikipedia, Wave, 2017, *Wave (gesture) – Wikipedia,* The Free Encyclopedia, from https://en.wikipedia.org/w/index.php?title=Wave_(gesture)&oldid=805051729.

Biographical Sketches

Dr.-Ing. Tobias F. Nowack

Affiliation: Technische Universität Ilmenau, Thüringer Innovationszentrum Mobilität, Ehrenbergstraße 15, D-98693 Ilmenau

Education:

1997 – 2004	Technische Universität Ilmenau: Media Technology (Dipl.-Ing.)
2017	Technische Universität Ilmenau: Doctoral degree (Dr.-Ing.)

Research and Professional Experience:

2004 – 2017	Technische Universität Ilmenau: Researcher in Ergonomics

Professional Appointments:

Since 2017	Technische Universität Ilmenau: Technical Staff in Antenna and High Frequency Measurement

Publications:

Nowack, T. & Dutschmann, C., 2017, 'Identify pointing and waving in gesture-based Human-Machine-Interaction,' *Engineering for a changing world*: 59th IWK, *Ilmenau Scientific Colloquium*, Technische Universität Ilmenau, 11th-15th September 2017: proceedings 2017.

Nowack, T. & Kurtz, P., 2017, *Mensch-Technik-Interaktion mittels Freiraumgesten',* Dissertationsschrift, Technische Universität Ilmenau, Germany [*Human-Technique Interaction via Free Space Gestures*', Dissertations, Technical University Ilmenau, Germany].

Nowack, T., Lutherdt, S., Witte, H. & Kurtz, P., 2017, *Nutzung von Zeigegesten für die körperliche Entlastung älterer Arbeitnehmer Prävention von arbeitsbedingten Gesundheitsgefahren und Erkrankungen* [*Use of pointers for the physical relief of older workers' Prevention of work-related health hazards and diseases*]: 23. Erfurter Tage, pp. 331–338, Verlag Bussert & Stadeler, Jena, Germany.

Nowack, T., Lutherdt, S., Jehring, S., Yue, X., Wenzel, S. & Kurtz, P., 2017, 'Detecting Deictic Gestures for Control of Mobile Robots,' in P. Savage-Knepshield and J. Chen (eds.), Advances in human factors in robots and unmanned systems, *Proceedings of the AHFE 2016 International Conference on Human Factors in Robots and Unmanned Systems,* July 27-31, 2016, Walt Disney World, Florida, USA, pp. 87–96.

Nowack, T., Wenzel, S. & Kurtz, P., 2016, 'Technische Beschreibung einer dynamischen und einer statischen Variante der Zeigegeste,' Arbeit in komplexen Systemen - digital, vernetzt, human?!: *62. Kongress der Gesellschaft für Arbeitswissenschaft*, RWTH Aachen University, Institut für Arbeitswissenschaft (IAW) [Technical description of a dynamic and a static variant of the pointing gesture, 'work in complex systems - digital, networked, human?': *62nd Congress of the Society for Industrial Engineering*, RWTH Aachen University, Institute of Industrial Engineering (IAW)], 2.-4. März 2016, A.4.12, GfA-Press, Dortmund, Germany.

Nowack, T., Jehring, S. & Kurtz, P., 2015, 'Zeigen – Objektauswahl für ein industrielles Assistenzsystem zum Heben und Tragen von Kleinladungsträgern' ['Show - Object Selection for an Industrial Assistance System for Lifting and Carrying Small Load Carriers'], in C. Wienrich, T. O. Zander, & K. Gramann (eds.), *Berlin-Brandenburgische Akademie der Wissenschaften (BBAW)* [Trends in Neuroergonomics, *Berlin-Brandenburg Academy of Sciences (BBAW)*], 7. - 9. Oktober 2015, pp. 152–158.

Nowack, T. F., Lutherdt, S., Gassmann, C. & Kurtz, P., 2015, 'Überprüfung der Gültigkeit von Fitts 'Law auf Touchscreens', in C. Wienrich, T. O. Zander, & K. Gramann (eds.), *'Trends in Neuroergonomics', Berlin-Brandenburgische Akademie der Wissenschaften (BBAW)* [*Berlin-Brandenburg Academy of Sciences (BBAW)*], 7. - 9. Oktober 2015, pp. 119–125.

Nowack, T. F., Suzal, N., Lutherdt, S., Schürger, K., Jehring, S. & Witte, H., et al., 2015, 'Phases of Technical Gesture Recognition', in M. Kurosu (ed.), *Human-computer interaction: Interaction technologies: 17th International Conference*, HCI International 2015, Los Angeles, CA, USA, August 2-7, 2015, Proceedings, pp. 130–139.

Univ.-Prof. Dipl.-Ing. Dr. med. (habil.) Hartmut Witte

Affiliation: Technische Universität Ilmenau, Fakultät für Maschinenbau, Fachgebiet Biomechatronik, Max-Planck-Ring 12, D-98693 Ilmenau

Education:

1979 – 1984	Universität Dortmund: Mechanical Engineering
1984 – 1990	Ruhr-Universität Bochum: Human Medicine
1990 – 1995:	Specialist in Anatomy
1992	Ruhr-Universität Bochum: Doctoral degree (Dr. med.)

1998	Ruhr-Universität Bochum, Faculty of Medicine: Venia legendi

Research and Professional Experience:

1990 – 1997	Ruhr-Universität Bochum: Researcher in Anatomy
1997 – 2002	Friedrich-Schiller-Universität Jena: Assistant Professor in Zoology

Professional Appointments:

2002	Technische Universität Ilmenau: Elected Professor of Biomechatronics

Honors:

2007	Elected Member of Sächsische Akademie der Wissenschaften zu Leipzig

Publications:

ORCID: 0000-0001-6055-2921

INDEX

G

H

I

K

L

M

N

O

P

R

S

T

U

W